# UNIX FOR DUMMIES®

## Quick Reference

4th Edition

by Margaret Levine Young and
John R. Levine

IDG BOOKS WORLDWIDE

IDG Books Worldwide, Inc.
An International Data Group Company

Foster City, CA ✦ Chicago, IL ✦ Indianapolis, IN ✦ New York, NY

# UNIX® For Dummies® Quick Reference, 4th Edition

Published by
**IDG Books Worldwide, Inc.**
An International Data Group Company
919 E. Hillsdale Blvd.
Suite 400
Foster City, CA 94404
www.idgbooks.com (IDG Books Worldwide Web site)
www.dummies.com (Dummies Press Web site)



Library of Congress Catalog Card No.: 98-87106

ISBN: 0-7645-0420-7

Printed in the United States of America

10 9 8 7 6 5

4P/RU/RS/ZY/IN

Distributed in the United States by IDG Books Worldwide, Inc.

Distributed by Macmillan Canada for Canada; by Transworld Publishers Limited in the United Kingdom; by IDG Norge Books for Norway; by IDG Sweden Books for Sweden; by Woodslane Pty. Ltd. for Australia; by Woodslane (NZ) Ltd. for New Zealand; by Addison Wesley Longman Singapore Pte Ltd. for Singapore, Malaysia, Thailand, Indonesia and Korea; by Norma Comunicaciones S.A. for Colombia; by Intersoft for South Africa; by International Thomson Publishing for Germany, Austria and Switzerland; by Toppan Company Ltd. for Japan; by Distribuidora Cuspide for Argentina; by Livraria Cultura for Brazil; by Ediciencia S.A. for Ecuador; by Ediciones ZETA S.C.R. Ltda. for Peru; by WS Computer Publishing Corporation, Inc., for the Philippines; by Unalis Corporation for Taiwan; by Contemporanea de Ediciones for Venezuela; by Computer Book & Magazine Store for Puerto Rico; by Express Computer Distributors for the Caribbean and West Indies. Authorized Sales Agent: Anthony Rudkin Associates for the Middle East and North Africa.

For general information on IDG Books Worldwide's books in the U.S., please call our Consumer Customer Service department at 800-762-2974. For reseller information, including discounts and premium sales, please call our Reseller Customer Service department at 800-434-3422.

For information on where to purchase IDG Books Worldwide's books outside the U.S., please contact our International Sales department at 650-655-3200 or fax 650-655-3297.

For information on foreign language translations, please contact our Foreign & Subsidiary Rights department at 650-655-3021 or fax 650-655-3281.

For sales inquiries and special prices for bulk quantities, please contact our Sales department at 650-655-3200 or write to the address above.

For information on using IDG Books Worldwide's books in the classroom or for ordering examination copies, please contact our Educational Sales department at 800-434-2086 or fax 317-596-5499.

For press review copies, author interviews, or other publicity information, please contact our Public Relations department at 650-655-3000 or fax 650-655-3299.

For authorization to photocopy items for corporate, personal, or educational use, please contact Copyright Clearance Center, 222 Rosewood Drive, Danvers, MA 01923, or fax 978-750-4470.

# About the Authors

**Margaret Levine Young** and **John R. Levine** were members of a computer club in high school (this was before high school students, or even high schools, had computers). They came in contact with Theodor H. Nelson, the author of *Computer Lib/Dream Machines* and the inventor of hypertext, who fostered the idea that computers should not be taken seriously. He showed them that everyone can understand and use computers.

John wrote his first program in 1967 on an IBM 1130 (a computer roughly as powerful as your typical modern digital wristwatch, only more difficult to use). His first exposure to UNIX was while hanging out with friends in Princeton in 1974; he became an official UNIX system administrator at Yale in 1975. John began working part-time for Interactive Systems, the first commercial UNIX company, in 1977 and has been in and out of the UNIX biz ever since. He used to spend most of his time writing software, but now he mostly writes books (including *The Internet For Dummies, UNIX For Dummies,* and *Internet Secrets,* published by IDG Books Worldwide, Inc.) because it's more fun and he can do so at home in the tiny village of Trumansburg, New York. He also speaks on the Internet and related topics. He holds a B.A. and a Ph.D. in computer science from Yale University, but please don't hold that against him. Gluttons for punishment can find out more at `http://iecc.com/johnl`.

Margy has been using small computers since the 1970s. She graduated from UNIX on a PDP/11 to Apple DOS on an Apple II to MS-DOS and UNIX on a variety of machines. She has done all kinds of jobs that involve explaining to people that computers aren't as mysterious as they might think, including managing the use of PCs at Columbia Pictures, teaching scientists and engineers what computers are good for, and writing computer manuals. She has been president of NYUPC, the New York PC Users Group. Margy has cowritten over a dozen computer books, including *The Internet For Dummies, WordPerfect 8 For Windows For Dummies,* and *Dummies 101: The Internet for Windows 95.* She has a degree in computer science from Yale University.

**Dave Guertin** (who updated this book for the 4th edition) came into the computer business via the back door. Unlike some other authors he can think of, he did not start playing with UNIX as a young nerd; instead, he waited until he was an older, established nerd. Dave began serious programming as a graduate student in zoology, writing programs that taxed the capabilities of the most powerful personal computer then available. To circumvent this problem, he ignored the skepticism of his peers and installed a fledgling operating system called Linux. He never looked back, and with the enthusiasm of the converted has used UNIX in his work ever since. Dave is currently the science specialist in Instructional Technology at Middlebury College, where he supports UNIX computing in the sciences.

# ABOUT IDG BOOKS WORLDWIDE

Welcome to the world of IDG Books Worldwide.

IDG Books Worldwide, Inc., is a subsidiary of International Data Group, the world's largest publisher of computer-related information and the leading global provider of information services on information technology. IDG was founded more than 25 years ago and now employs more than 8,500 people worldwide. IDG publishes more than 275 computer publications in over 75 countries (see listing below). More than 90 million people read one or more IDG publications each month.

Launched in 1990, IDG Books Worldwide is today the #1 publisher of best-selling computer books in the United States. We are proud to have received eight awards from the Computer Press Association in recognition of editorial excellence and three from *Computer Currents*' First Annual Readers' Choice Awards. Our best-selling *...For Dummies®* series has more than 50 million copies in print with translations in 38 languages. IDG Books Worldwide, through a joint venture with IDG's Hi-Tech Beijing, became the first U.S. publisher to publish a computer book in the People's Republic of China. In record time, IDG Books Worldwide has become the first choice for millions of readers around the world who want to learn how to better manage their businesses.

Our mission is simple: Every one of our books is designed to bring extra value and skill-building instructions to the reader. Our books are written by experts who understand and care about our readers. The knowledge base of our editorial staff comes from years of experience in publishing, education, and journalism — experience we use to produce books for the '90s. In short, we care about books, so we attract the best people. We devote special attention to details such as audience, interior design, use of icons, and illustrations. And because we use an efficient process of authoring, editing, and desktop publishing our books electronically, we can spend more time ensuring superior content and spend less time on the technicalities of making books.

You can count on our commitment to deliver high-quality books at competitive prices on topics you want to read about. At IDG Books Worldwide, we continue in the IDG tradition of delivering quality for more than 25 years. You'll find no better book on a subject than one from IDG Books Worldwide.

IDG BOOKS WORLDWIDE

John Kilcullen
CEO
IDG Books Worldwide, Inc.

Steven Berkowitz
President and Publisher
IDG Books Worldwide, Inc.

VIII WINNER — *Eighth Annual Computer Press Awards 1992*

IX WINNER — *Ninth Annual Computer Press Awards 1993*

1995 COMPUTER CURRENTS READERS' CHOICE

X WINNER — *Tenth Annual Computer Press Awards 1994*

XI WINNER — *Eleventh Annual Computer Press Awards 1995*

IDG Books Worldwide, Inc., is a subsidiary of International Data Group, the world's largest publisher of computer-related information and the leading global provider of information services on information technology. International Data Group publishes over 275 computer publications in over 75 countries. More than 90 million people read one or more International Data Group publications each month. International Data Group's publications include: **ARGENTINA:** Buyer's Guide, Computerworld Argentina, PC World Argentina; **AUSTRALIA:** Australian Macworld, Australian PC World, Australian Reseller News, Computerworld, IT Casebook, Network World, Publish, Webmaster; **AUSTRIA:** Computerwelt Osterreich, Networks Austria, PC Tip Austria; **BANGLADESH:** PC World Bangladesh; **BELARUS:** PC World Belarus; **BELGIUM:** Data News; **BRAZIL:** Annuário de Informática, Computerworld, Connections, Macworld, PC Player, PC World, Publish, Reseller News, Supergamepower; **BULGARIA:** Computerworld Bulgaria, Network World Bulgaria, PC & MacWorld Bulgaria; **CANADA:** CIO Canada, Client/Server World, ComputerWorld Canada, InfoWorld Canada, NetworkWorld Canada, WebWorld; **CHILE:** Computerworld Chile, PC World Chile; **COLOMBIA:** Computerworld Colombia, PC World Colombia; **COSTA RICA:** PC World Centro America; **THE CZECH AND SLOVAK REPUBLICS:** Computerworld Czechoslovakia, Macworld Czech Republic, PC World Czechoslovakia; **DENMARK:** Communications World Danmark, Computerworld Danmark, Macworld Danmark, PC World Danmark, Techworld Denmark; **DOMINICAN REPUBLIC:** PC World Republica Dominicana; **ECUADOR:** PC World Ecuador; **EGYPT:** Computerworld Middle East, PC World Middle East; **EL SALVADOR:** PC World Centro America; **FINLAND:** MikroPC, Tietoverkko, Tietoviikko; **FRANCE:** Distributique, Hebdo, Info PC, Le Monde Informatique, Macworld, Reseaux & Telecoms, WebMaster France; **GERMANY:** Computer Partner, Computerwoche, Computerwoche Extra, Computerwoche FOCUS, Global Online, Macwelt, PC Welt; **GREECE:** Amiga Computing, GamePro Greece, Multimedia World; **GUATEMALA:** PC World Centro America; **HONDURAS:** PC World Centro America; **HONG KONG:** Computerworld Hong Kong, PC World Hong Kong, Publish in Asia; **HUNGARY:** ABCD CD-ROM, Computerworld Szamitastechnika, Internetto online Magazine, PC World Hungary, PC-X Magazin Hungary; **ICELAND:** Tolvuheimur PC World Island; **INDIA:** Information Communications World, Information Systems Computerworld, PC World India, Publish in Asia; **INDONESIA:** InfoKomputer PC World, Komputek Computerworld, Publish in Asia; **IRELAND:** ComputerScope, PC Live!; **ISRAEL:** Macworld Israel, People & Computers/Computerworld; **ITALY:** Computerworld Italia, Macworld Italia, Networking Italia, PC World Italia; **JAPAN:** DTP World, Macworld Japan, Nikkei Personal Computing, OS/2 World Japan, SunWorld Japan, Windows NT World, Windows World Japan; **KENYA:** PC World East African; **KOREA:** Hi-Tech Information, Macworld Korea, PC World Korea; **MACEDONIA:** PC World Macedonia; **MALAYSIA:** Computerworld Malaysia, PC World Malaysia, Publish in Asia; **MALTA:** PC World Malta; **MEXICO:** Computerworld Mexico, PC World Mexico; **MYANMAR:** PC World Myanmar; **NETHERLANDS:** Computer! Totaal, LAN Internetworking Magazine, LAN World Buyers Guide, Macworld Netherlands, Net, WebWereld; **NEW ZEALAND:** Absolute Beginners Guide and Plain & Simple Series, Computer Buyer, Computer Industry Directory, Computerworld New Zealand, MTB, Network World, PC World New Zealand; **NICARAGUA:** PC World Centro America; **NORWAY:** Computerworld Norge, CW Rapport, Datamagasinet, Financial Rapport, Kursguide Norge, Macworld Norge, Multimediaworld Norge, PC World Ekspress Norge, PC World Nettverk, PC World Norge, PC World ProduktGuide Norge; **PAKISTAN:** Computerworld Pakistan; **PANAMA:** PC World Panama; **PEOPLE'S REPUBLIC OF CHINA:** China Computer Users, China Computerworld, China InfoWorld, China Telecom World Weekly, Computer & Communication, Electronic Design China, Electronics Today, Electronics Weekly, Game Software, PC World China, Popular Computer Week, Software Weekly, Software World, Telecom World; **PERU:** Computerworld Peru, PC World Profesional Peru, PC World SoHo Peru; **PHILIPPINES:** Click!, Computerworld Philippines, PC World Philippines, Publish in Asia; **POLAND:** Computerworld Poland, Computerworld Special Report Poland, Cyber, Macworld Poland, Networld Poland, PC World Komputer; **PORTUGAL:** Cerebro/PC World, Computerworld/Correio Informático, Dealer World Portugal, Mac*In/PC*In Portugal, Multimedia World; **PUERTO RICO:** PC World Puerto Rico; **ROMANIA:** Computerworld Romania, PC World Romania, Telecom Romania; **RUSSIA:** Computerworld Russia, Mir PK, Publish, Seti; **SINGAPORE:** Computerworld Singapore, PC World Singapore, Publish in Asia; **SLOVENIA:** Monitor; **SOUTH AFRICA:** Computing SA, Network World SA, Software World SA; **SPAIN:** Communicaciones World España, Computerworld España, Dealer World España, Macworld España, PC World España; **SRI LANKA:** Infolink PC World; **SWEDEN:** CAP&Design, Computer Sweden, Corporate Computing Sweden, Internetworld Sweden, it.branschen, Macworld Sweden, MaxiData Sweden, MikroDatorn, Nätverk & Kommunikation, PC World Sweden, PCaktiv, Windows World Sweden; **SWITZERLAND:** Computerworld Schweiz, Macworld Schweiz, PCtip; **TAIWAN:** Computerworld Taiwan, Macworld Taiwan, NEW ViSiON/Publish, PC World Taiwan, Windows World Taiwan; **THAILAND:** Publish in Asia, Thai Computerworld; **TURKEY:** Computerworld Turkiye, Macworld Turkiye, Network World Turkiye, PC World Turkiye; **UKRAINE:** Computerworld Kiev, Multimedia World Ukraine, PC World Ukraine; **UNITED KINGDOM:** Acorn User UK, Amiga Action UK, Amiga Computing UK, Apple Talk UK, Computing, Macworld, Parents and Computers UK, PC Advisor, PC Home, PSX Pro, The WEB; **UNITED STATES:** Cable in the Classroom, CIO Magazine, Computerworld, DOS World, Federal Computer Week, GamePro Magazine, InfoWorld, I-Way, Macworld, Network World, PC Games, PC World, Publish, Video Event, THE WEB Magazine, and WebMaster; online webzines: JavaWorld, NetscapeWorld, and SunWorld Online; **URUGUAY:** InfoWorld Uruguay; **VENEZUELA:** Computerworld Venezuela, PC World Venezuela; and **VIETNAM:** PC World Vietnam.

5/7/98

Authors' Acknowledgments

John, Margy, and Dave would like to acknowledge Tim Gallan and Stephanie Koutek for their fine editing and Joshua and Stephen Pedrick for their outstanding technical review. In addition, Margy would like to thank her husband Jordan, Joyce Newton, and the Cornwall Elementary School for making it possible for her to get any work done.

## Publisher's Acknowledgments

We're proud of this book; please register your comments through our IDG Books Worldwide Online Registration Form located at `http://my2cents.dummies.com`.

Some of the people who helped bring this book to market include the following:

***Acquisitions, Editorial, and Media Development***

**Senior Project Editor:** Tim Gallan

**Acquisitions Editor:** Michael Kelly

**Copy Editor:** Stephanie Koutek

**Technical Reviewers:** Joshua Pedrick and Stephen Pedrick

**Editorial Manager:** Lean P. Cameron

**Media Development Manager:** Heather Heath Dismore

**Editorial Assistant:** Donna Love

***Production***

**Project Coordinator:** E. Shawn Aylsworth

**Layout and Graphics:** Lou Boudreau, Drew R. Moore, Kate Snell

**Proofreaders:** Christine Berman, Kelli Botta, Rachel Garvey, Nancy Price, Janet M. Withers

**Indexer:** Nancy Anderman Guenther

***General and Administrative***

**IDG Books Worldwide, Inc.:** John Kilcullen, CEO; Steven Berkowitz, President and Publisher

**IDG Books Technology Publishing:** Brenda McLaughlin, Senior Vice President and Group Publisher

**Dummies Technology Press and Dummies Editorial:** Diane Graves Steele, Vice President and Associate Publisher; Mary Bednarek, Director of Acquisitions and Product Development; Kristin A. Cocks, Editorial Director

**Dummies Trade Press:** Kathleen A. Welton, Vice President and Publisher; Kevin Thornton, Acquisitions Manager

**IDG Books Production for Dummies Press:** Michael R. Britton, Vice President of Production and Creative Services; Cindy L. Phipps, Manager of Project Coordination, Production Proofreading, and Indexing; Kathie S. Schutte, Supervisor of Page Layout; Shelley Lea, Supervisor of Graphics and Design; Debbie J. Gates, Production Systems Specialist; Robert Springer, Supervisor of Proofreading; Debbie Stailey, Special Projects Coordinator; Tony Augsburger, Supervisor of Reprints and Bluelines

**Dummies Packaging and Book Design:** Robin Seaman, Creative Director; Kavish + Kavish, Cover Design

♦

The publisher would like to give special thanks to Patrick J. McGovern, without whom this book would not have been possible.

♦

# Table of Contents

Intro

# How to Use This Book

At last, a UNIX reference book that includes only the tasks and commands you might conceivably have some interest in! In this book, you can find information about lots of UNIX commands — more than 100 — and how to use them. But we leave out the other 10 zillion commands and options that only nerds love.

We also include information about several widely used parts of UNIX: X Window managers; the `ed`, `emacs`, `pico`, and `vi` text editors; electronic mail; and networking. Don't flip through lots of confusing manuals to find that command you're looking for — just check out the relevant part of this book. The table of contents and the extensive index should help you find whatever you need.

# What's in This Book

This book is divided into eight sections so that you can find things quickly.

Part I, "Commanding UNIX Using the Shell," has information about how to type commands, name files and directories, and use pipes and filters.

Part II, "UNIX Commands," contains our favorite 100 or so UNIX commands with the options you're likely to use. We include examples and warnings when necessary.

Part III, "Using X Window Managers," was written for people who use UNIX's most popular window managers, Motif and FVWM, and the Common Desktop Environment (CDE).

Part IV, "Using Text Editors (ed, emacs, pico, and vi)," contains command summaries for these four editors.

Part V, "Sending and Receiving Electronic Mail," has instructions for using several different mail programs to handle your electronic mail.

Part VI, "Connecting to Other Computers," contains commands for accessing computers on a network.

Part VII, "Finding Resources on the Net," contains instructions for finding information on networks, including the Internet.

And Part VIII, "Usenet Newsgroups," describes Usenet, the global networked bulletin board system.

There's also a glossary at the end of the book that you can use to look up the terms that you have forgotten or that are just plain baffling to you.

# Conventions Used in This Book

When you have to type something, it appears in boldface, like this: Type **elm**. When we want you to type something longer, it appears like this:

```
terribly important UNIX command
```

Be sure to type it just as it appears. Use the same capitalization we do, because UNIX considers the capital and lowercase versions of the same letter to be totally different beasts. Then press the Enter or Return key.

In the text, UNIX commands and filenames are shown `in this typeface`.

Part II contains a cryptic "UNIXspeak" version of each command, showing all its options and arguments. Information in **boldface** is required when you're using the command. Stuff in [square brackets] is optional, so try leaving it out. Text in *italics* represents information that you provide; if you see *filename,* for example, fill in the name of the file you want to work with. (Don't worry; we explain it all later.)

# The Cast of Icons

For each command or task that we describe — and whenever we provide other important information — we include icons that tell you about what you're reading.

TIP: A tip that can save you time or impress your local UNIX guru.

WARNING: Watch out! Something about this command or task can cause trouble for you.

WEIRDNESS: Who knows why, but this command or task may not work as you would typically expect.

NETWORK: A command or task that's useful if your computer is connected to a network. If not, don't use it!

CROSS-REFERENCE: A handy cross-reference to the chapters in *UNIX For Dummies,* 4th Edition, and other related *...For Dummies* books that cover this topic in more detail.

# Write to Us!

If you have an opinion about this book (or if you want to test your e-mail), write to the authors at `unixqr4@gurus.com`. For updates to this book, check our Web site at `net.gurus.com`.

You can contact IDG Books Worldwide, Inc., the publisher, about this or other *...For Dummies* books by writing to `info@idgbooks.com`. Check out the Dummies Web site at `www.dummies.com`.

Part I

# Commanding UNIX Using the Shell

We work from the outside in, so the shell sounds like a good place to begin. (If this statement makes you think that UNIX resembles an insect, only not as attractive, know that we think along the same lines.) The *shell* program reads your commands and processes them.

Several UNIX shells are available. The most popular are Bourne, C, BASH, and Korn, all of which we describe in this part. Some of these shells have extra commands that the others don't, and the syntax of the commands may differ slightly between shells, but they all act essentially the same.

Unless you're the victim — er, beneficiary — of a fancy graphical interface, you communicate with UNIX by typing commands. Here, we discuss what commands look like and some general rules that apply to all commands. Even if you have a graphical interface, you will end up typing shell commands into a window, so you'll need some of this information anyway.

## In this part . . .

- **Entering commands**
- **Understanding how information is organized in files and directories**
- **Using wildcard characters to specify files you want to process**
- **Determining which shell you are using**
- **Getting help**

# Directories

A *directory* is a special kind of file that contains the names of other files and directories. All files are arranged in directories. (Macs and Windows PCs use the term *folders* for directories, but they are the same thing.)

At any given moment, one directory is the *current directory* (or *working directory*) of files you are using right now. When you first log in, your current directory is your *home directory* (or *login directory*), which the system administrator made for you.

You can — and usually should — make other directories in which to store files for various projects. You can switch to other directories with the `cd` command, make new directories with `mkdir`, and get rid of directories you no longer want with `rmdir`. (***See*** the entries for these commands in Part II.)

- In the C, BASH, and Korn shells, the ~ (tilde) is shorthand for your home directory. For example, if your home directory is `/home/elvis`, then `~/hits` is the same as `/home/elvis/hits`.
- As with filenames, you can use uppercase and lowercase letters, digits, periods, and underscores in your directory names. UNIX considers uppercase and lowercase to be different.

TIP

A good general rule is to use all lowercase for files and initial capital letters for directories.

# Environment Variables

Every UNIX shell has *shell variables,* which are short names for chunks of text. Some shell variables can be *environment variables,* which are available to programs run from the shell. You can make your own variables if you want.

The most useful environment variables are listed in the following table:

| *Variable* | *What It Contains* |
|---|---|
| HOME | Pathname of your home directory (for example, `/home/john`) |
| LOGNAME | Your username (for example, `fredz`) |
| PATH | List of directories in which the shell looks for programs |

To refer to a shell variable by name, type a dollar sign before it. Because the variable HOME automatically contains the name of your home directory, for example, type this:

```
echo $HOME
```

You see something like this:

```
/home/elvis
```

You can use variable names within quoted text. For example, you may want to display your username within text that includes spaces, so you need to enclose the spaces in quotes. Type this:

```
echo "My login name is $LOGNAME."
```

You see something like this:

```
My login name is elvis.
```

To see a list of all the shell variables, type **set**. To see all the environment variables, type **env** on System V or **printenv** on BSD.

# Filenames

Information that you save is stored in files. Each file has a name. (Actually, each file can have many names — ***see*** the `ln` entry in Part II.) You can use letters, digits, periods, hyphens, and underscores in filenames. (You can use other characters as well, but stick to these to avoid confusion.) Uppercase and lowercase are different, so `tadpole`, `TadPole`, and `TADPOLE` are different names.

Don't use odd characters in filenames, such as / ! @ # $ ^ & * - ( ) + ‘ “ \ | ? Also, don't use spaces in filenames. Most programs won't let you, anyway. Use periods or underlines to string words together, like this:

```
squid_soup_recipe
```

# Help with Commands

If you need help with a UNIX command, you can display the online reference manual by using the `man` (for *manual*) command. Simply type **man**, followed by the name of the command you need information about.

If you have forgotten the options that you can use with the `ls` command, for example, type this:

```
man ls
```

TIP

On some systems, the manual page flies by too quickly to read. You can force it to display a page at a time by running the output through the `more` command. Type this:

```
man ls | more
```

CROSS-REFERENCE

***See also*** *UNIX For Dummies,* 4th Edition (published by IDG Books Worldwide, Inc.). You can find more detailed information about shells and commands in Chapter 2 and about files and directories in Chapters 5 and 6. Chapter 7 of *MORE UNIX For Dummies* (IDG Books Worldwide, Inc.) covers startup commands.

# Identifying Your Shell

Here's a handy way to find out which shell you're using. Type the following line:

```
echo $RANDOM
```

and then press the Enter key. If you get a blank line, it's the *Bourne shell (sh).* If you get the following line:

```
RANDOM: Undefined variable
```

it's the *C shell (csh* or *tcsh).* If you get a five-digit random number, it's the *Korn shell* (*ksh*) or *BASH.* To tell ksh from BASH, type

```
help
```

If you get a page of command descriptions, you have BASH. If not, you have the Korn shell.

TIP

The Korn and BASH shells are extended versions of the Bourne shell, so all three use nearly the same syntax. The C shell, on the other hand, was written thousands of miles from the other three and looks it.

# Pathnames

A *pathname,* or *path,* tells UNIX how to find the particular file you want. If you use a plain filename (`tadpole`, for example), UNIX understands it as a file in the current directory. You refer to files in other directories by using a list of names strung together with slashes. Typing the name **snacks/tadpole** tells UNIX to look in the current directory for a subdirectory called `snacks` and to look there for a file called `tadpole`.

If the path begins with a slash, it's an *absolute path,* or one that starts from the root of the file system. A typical absolute path is `/usr/elvis/songs/hound_dog`. An absolute path always means the same thing, regardless of what your current directory is.

# Quoting Characters on the Command Line

Sometimes you have to use special characters in your commands. For example, to list filenames that have a question mark in them, you need to tell the shell that the question mark you're typing should *not* be interpreted as a wildcard character. This is called *quoting* the character.

To quote any special character, including a space, precede it with a backslash (\). You can even type \\ to quote a backslash. For example, to list filenames that contain a question mark, type this:

```
ls *\?*
```

Single and double quotation marks quote strings of characters. They must match correctly. Single quotes are more potent than double quotes. Everything between double quotes is taken literally, even backslashes, with the following caveats:

- ✦ Wildcard characters (like * and ?) are taken literally; that is, they don't match groups of filenames.
- ✦ Dollar-sign variable names are replaced by their values.
- ✦ You can quote double quotes in single quotes and vice versa.

For example, to display the text "Too #&@!;) much punctuation!" on-screen, you can use the `echo` command like this:

```
echo "Too #&@!;) much punctuation!"
```

TIP: If the last character on a line is a backslash, it means that the command continues on the next line.

# Redirecting with Pipes and Filters

Every command has *standard input* and *standard output.* They are normally your keyboard and screen, respectively. You can tell the shell to redirect the input or output of any command.

| *Redirection Character* | *What It Does* |
|---|---|
| > | Redirects the output of a command to a file or device, replacing previous contents (if any). |
| >> | Redirects the output of a command, adding it to the existing file, if there is one. |
| < | Redirects the input of a command from a file or device. |
| \| | Sends (pipes) the output of one command to become the input of another command. |

For example, to store a listing of files in `myfiles`, type this:

```
ls -l > myfiles
```

To append the listing to the end of an existing file, type this:

```
ls -l >> myfiles
```

To sort the contents of the file `mydata` and display the results, type this:

```
sort < mydata
```

To sort `mydata` and produce `mysorteddata`, type this:

```
sort < mydata > mysorteddata
```

You can redirect the output of one program into the input of another by using a *pipe,* which is written as a vertical bar (|). To make a file listing and send it to the printer, type this:

```
ls -l | lpr
```

You can pipe together as many programs as you want. To make a file listing, add headings with `pr` and print the result:

```
ls -l | pr -h "my files" | lpr
```

Programs that are usually used with redirection are called *filters.* The filters you are most likely to run into are `more`, `sort`, and maybe `tee`. ***See*** the entries for these filters in Part II.

WARNING: Redirecting output to a file using the > character blows away the previous contents of the file and replaces it with the output of the command. To prevent file loss, use >> to redirect output instead.

## Shell Prompts

The shell tells you that it's ready for you to type a command by displaying a prompt string, usually a percent sign (%) for the C shell and a dollar sign ($) for the other shells. Some systems are set up with more complex prompts, including the terminal name, directory name, and so on.

# Special Characters and What They Do

Nearly every punctuation character means something special to the shell. Unfortunately, the characters vary from system to system. (You can use the `stty` command to change these characters; ***see*** the entry for `stty` in Part II.) This section presents a roundup of the most useful special characters.

| *Special Character* | *What It Does* |
|---|---|
| Enter or Return | Ends a line you're typing. |
| Spacebar or Tab | Separates words in commands. |
| Backspace, Delete, or Ctrl+H | Backspaces over errors. If none of these characters work, try # (and use `stty` to change it to something else, if you prefer). |
| ; | Separates two commands on the same line. |
| & | After a command, tells the shell to run that command in the background and immediately return for another command. (***See*** `bg`, `fg`, and `kill` in Part II for commands to control background programs.) A pair of ampersands (&&) is an obscure way to perform the command following the && only if the one preceding the && *succeeded.* |
| \| | Between two commands, splices the output of the first command to the input of the second, creating a *pipeline.* (***See*** the section "Redirecting with Pipes and Filters," earlier in this part.) A pair of vertical bars (\|\|) is an obscure way to perform the command following the \|\| only if the one preceding the \|\| *failed.* |
| ! | In the C and BASH shells, repeats a previously typed command, identified by what follows the !. Other than !!, which repeats the preceding command, avoid exclamation points (in the C shell and BASH only). |
| # | Whatever comment follows the # is ignored by the shell. |
| \ | At the end of a line, indicates that the command is continued on the next line. Anywhere else, \ quotes the following character so that it isn't treated as a special character. (***See*** the section "Quoting Characters on the Command Line," earlier in this part.) |

*(continued)*

| *Special Character* | *What It Does* |
|---|---|
| ' or " | Quotes a group of characters so that they aren't treated as special characters. (***See*** the section "Quoting Characters on the Command Line," earlier in this part.) |
| $ | Introduces a reference to a variable. (***See*** "Environment Variables," earlier in this part.) |
| ? | Wildcard that matches any single character. (***See*** "Wildcards," later in this part.) |
| * | Wildcard that matches any number of characters. (***See*** "Wildcards," later in this part.) |
| [ ] | Contains a group of characters to be used as wildcards. (***See*** "Wildcards," later in this part.) |
| Ctrl+C | Stops programs that are stuck. If possible, use the program's `exit` command or the equivalent. Some programs, particularly text editors, catch Ctrl+C and wait for you to type another command. You can also try pressing the Delete key if Ctrl+C doesn't work. |
| Ctrl+D | Marks the end of input when you're typing directly to a program. |
| Ctrl+U or Ctrl+X | Cancels the line you're typing and starts over. If neither of these works, try @ (and use the `stty` command to change it to something more friendly). |
| Ctrl+Z | Pauses the program you're running and returns to the shell. Use the commands `fg`, `bg`, and `kill` to restart or stop the program. Some older shells do not support Ctrl+Z. (***See*** the entries for the `fg`, `bg`, and `kill` commands in Part II.) |

If you don't want to remember all this punctuation, just don't use special characters.

To use special characters in commands as if they were normal characters, quote them. (***See*** the section "Quoting Characters on the Command Line," earlier in this part.)

WARNING

- ✦ Most shells interpret Ctrl+D as a command to log you out. So don't press it when you see the shell prompt. To terminate the program you're running, try Ctrl+C or Delete (if Delete doesn't act as your backspace key).
- ✦ Even though your keyboard has arrow keys and the cursor moves as it should when you press them, the only programs that understand them are full-screen text editors, such as `emacs` and `vi` and a few of the more modern shells, including BASH and tcsh.
- ✦ Do not confuse the Backspace key, which usually works everywhere, with the left-arrow key, which works only in full-screen editors and BASH.

# Startup Files

System settings are stored in special files. These files contain information such as the following:

- ✦ The type of display you're using
- ✦ The way your keyboard functions
- ✦ The default text editor
- ✦ What, if any, commands run automatically when you log in

These files are normally hidden because the filenames begin with a period. To view a list of these files, type this:

```
ls -d .*
```

The important startup files for each UNIX shell are shown in the following table.

| *Shell* | *Startup Files* |
|---|---|
| csh, tcsh | .cshrc, .login |
| ksh, sh | .profile |
| bash | .bashrc, .profile |

You can customize these files by using a text editor. Because the commands in these files vary depending on which shell you're using and the way your system is set up, we do not describe them here.

You shouldn't need to change these files unless you're having a problem, such as seeing strange characters when you type. See your system administrator if you need to change your environment.

# Typing Commands

Issuing a command consists of typing a series of words and then pressing the Enter (or Return) key. The first word is the name of the command, and the rest of the words are *arguments* that affect the way the command works. If the command to remove a file is `rm`, for example, the arguments specify which file to remove. All standard UNIX command names are lowercase, so you generally type commands in lowercase.

TIP: Commands can be as long as you want. If you type a command that doesn't fit on a line, just keep typing, and UNIX continues it on the next line. It may look like two lines on-screen, but until you press Enter, the computer thinks that it's one line.

# Wildcards

Often, you want a command to operate on a group of files with similar names. The shell lets you use special wildcard characters to specify a group of files. This table shows the three primary kinds of wildcards:

| *Wildcard Character* | *What It Does* |
|---|---|
| ? | Matches any single character. |
| * | Matches any number of characters. |
| [ ] | Matches any one of the letters in the brackets. |

For example, **h*** indicates all the files in the current directory that begin with an *h*; **h*g** indicates all the files that begin with *h* and end with *g*; **part[123]** indicates files named `part1`, `part2`, and `part3`; **part[0-9]** indicates all of `part0` through `part9`; and ***** indicates every file in the directory. As a special case, wildcards don't match a name that starts with a period unless you explicitly type the period.

TIP: Unlike those on some PC systems, UNIX wildcards do the right thing even when you use directories. For example, ***/*c** means all files that end with the letter *c* in subdirectories of the current directory.

Wildcards are handled by the shell itself, not by the command you're running. This means that all commands handle wildcards in exactly the same way. However, even when part of a command isn't a filename or when it has stars or question marks or brackets, the shell tries to make filenames out of it unless you quote it. (***See*** the section "Quoting Characters on the Command Line," earlier in this part.)

TIP: Predicting how wildcards may work is not always easy. Before you do something dangerous with them, like delete a bunch of files, use the `ls` command to see which filenames your wildcards match.

Part II

# UNIX Commands

If it weren't for commands, UNIX wouldn't be that hard to use, really. But `grep`? `awk`? These words don't sound like commands — they sound like intestinal noises.

Because UNIX, used from the shell, is a text-based system, though, you have to communicate with the system by typing commands. UNIX has zillions of commands, and we have selected the ones that either you may want to use yourself or a UNIX guru may tell you to use.

## In this part . . .

- **This part lists the most useful UNIX commands. Some commands have numerous options that are rarely used, so we tell you about just the ones you're likely to run into.**
- **For each command, we include a "UNIXspeak" section that shows all the options and arguments you may have to use. In this section, information in bold is required when using the command. Text in [square brackets] is optional, so you can usually leave it out. Text in *italics* represents information that you must provide; for example, where you see *filename*, you fill in the name of the file you want to work with. (Don't type filename!)**

# alias

Creates an alias for a command or shows which aliases exist (C, BASH, and Korn shells only).

## UNIXspeak (C shell)

```
alias [name ['command']]
```

## UNIXspeak (Korn and BASH shells)

```
alias [name=['command']]
```

| Option or Argument | Function |
|---|---|
| *name* | Specifies the alias name. |
| *command* | Specifies the command the name should be an alias for. |

## Sample

You don't want to type a long command that you use often. Instead, you want to assign it a short nickname, or *alias.* You may be tired of typing **ls -l**, for example, and would rather just press *d* to see the files in your directory.

If you use the C shell, type

```
alias d 'ls -l'
```

If you use the BASH or Korn shell, type

```
alias d='ls -l'
```

You have just created a new command, `d`, which is the same as `ls -l`.

To see which aliases you have defined, just type

```
alias
```

Aliases that you create are not saved when you log out. However, you can add the alias commands that define them to your startup files so that they run automatically when you log in. ***See*** "Startup Files" in Part I for details.

# at

Schedules a command to be run at a particular time. This command is great for running time-consuming commands later, such as in the middle of the night.

## UNIXspeak

```
at [-f filename] [-m] time [date]
```

or

```
at -l
```

or

```
at -r job
```

| Option or Argument | Function |
|---|---|
| -f *filename* | Specifies the name of the file that contains the command (or commands) to run. |
| -m | Sends you an electronic-mail message after the command has been run. |
| *time* | Indicates when you want the command to run. Type the time in the format *hh:mm* followed by **am** or **pm**, or you can use a 24-hour clock. You can type **midnight** to run your command at midnight or **now +** followed by the number of minutes or hours (for example, **now + 6 hours**). |
| *date* | Indicates on which day you want the command to run. Type the date in the *month day, year* format, where *month* is the name of the month (such as **Dec** or **December**, not 12), *day* is the day (such as **25**), and *year* is the four-digit year (such as **1999**). You need the year only if the date is more than 12 months in the future. |
| -l | Lists the names of commands (jobs) that you have already scheduled. Don't type anything on the command line after `-l`. |
| -r *job* | Cancels a command (job) that you previously scheduled. Type the job number after `-r`. To find out the job number, use the `-l` option. |

## Sample

You want to print a huge document during the night. Type

```
at midnight
```

After you press Enter, UNIX doesn't display a prompt. Instead, it waits for you to type the commands that you want to run at midnight. Type this:

```
lpr big.report
```

Press Enter again and then press Ctrl+D when you're finished.

After you schedule a job, you can check that `at` hasn't forgotten about it. Type

```
at -l
```

You see a list of your scheduled jobs with their job numbers. If you decide to cancel one — for example, the job whose number is 753460300.a — type

```
at -r 753460300.a
```

Your system administrator can control who is allowed to use `at`. If you're not on the list, `at` tells you so when you try to use it.

***See also*** `crontab`.

# awk

A strange programming language used by UNIX nerds to perform an amazing array of tasks.

## UNIXspeak

```
awk [-f program] file
```

| Option or Argument | Function |
|---|---|
| *-f* | Specifies that the filename that follows contains an `awk` program. |
| *program* | Specifies the name of the `awk` program to run. |
| *file* | Specifies the name of the file to modify by using the `awk` program or by serving as input to it. |

Other versions of `awk` are named `gawk` and `nawk`. They all work more or less the same. ***See*** Chapter 9 of *MORE UNIX For Dummies* (IDG Books Worldwide, Inc.) for more information about `awk` programming.

## Sample

Programs written in `awk` usually read one file (the input) and create another file (the output). If you keep your checkbook in a file, for example, one check to a line, creating an `awk` program to compute the current balance is easy.

# bash

Runs the Bourne Again shell.

When you use UNIX, you're always using a shell. The other shells are the Bourne shell (`sh`), the Korn shell (`ksh`), and the C shell (`csh` or `tcsh`). The `bash` command is most often useful to run a BASH script that someone has given you.

### UNIXspeak

```
bash [script]
```

| Option or Argument | Function |
|---|---|
| *script* | Name of a file that contains a BASH shell script. |

### Sample

A friend gives you a shell script named `fix.it.up` that you want to run. She tells you that the script works with BASH, so you run it by typing

```
bash fix.it.up
```

## bc

A handy desk calculator.

The `bc` calculator can do sophisticated computations, including square roots, trigonometry, conditional calculations, and conversions among hexadecimal, octal, and decimal numbers. You can even define your own functions.

### UNIXspeak

```
bc [file]
```

| Option or Argument | Function |
|---|---|
| *file* | Specifies the name of a file full of `bc` commands. If you want to multiply just a few numbers, leave out this option. |

### Sample

Type **bc**. Nothing is displayed, but the calculator is now running. Type

```
4500 * .67
```

to calculate a quick discount. Whew! `bc` displays the answer. When you're finished doing calculations, press Ctrl+D or type **quit**.

# bg

Continues a stopped job in the background. To find out which jobs are running in the background, type **jobs**.

To cancel a job that's running in the background, you use the `kill` command. To move a background job into the foreground, you use the `fg` command. (We describe both later in this part.)

Some versions of the Bourne and Korn shells don't have *job control,* which is the capability to run jobs in the background. If pressing Ctrl+Z doesn't stop a job, your shell doesn't have job control.

## UNIXspeak

```
bg [job]
```

| Option or Argument | Function |
| --- | --- |
| *job* | Specifies the job number that you want to run in the background. If you don't include the job number, UNIX assumes that you mean the current job. |

## Sample

You start a slow program (for example, compressing a very large file) and then decide that you want to run it in the background. You press Ctrl+Z to stop the job. UNIX says something like `Stopped`. To continue the job in the background and leave the foreground free for you to give other commands, type **bg**.

# cal

Prints a calendar for a month or a year.

If you type just **cal** with no month or year, you get the calendar for the current month. If you provide a year but no month, `cal` prints a 12-month calendar for the year.

To save the calendar in a text file rather than print it on-screen, redirect `cal`'s output to a file, like this:

```
cal 12 1995 > christmas.trip.calendar
```

Because `cal` can do calendars back to the year 1, typing **cal 95** prints a calendar for the year 95 A.D., not 1995, so watch out.

### UNIXspeak

```
cal [month] [year]
```

| *Option or Argument* | *Function* |
|---|---|
| *month* | Specifies the month (1 to 12) for which you want a calendar. |
| *year* | Specifies the year (1 to 9999) for which you want a calendar. |

### Sample

You're planning a trip for next March, but your desk calendar doesn't go that far into the future. Type

```
cal 3 1999
```

# calendar

Displays appointments and reminders for today.

If you use electronic mail, you don't have to run the `calendar` program. If you have a file named `calendar` in your home directory, most UNIX systems automagically run `calendar` every day at midnight and mail you the results. When you arrive in the morning, your reminders are in your mailbox.

### UNIXspeak

```
calendar
```

### Sample

To use the `calendar` program, you first need a `calendar` file. Use any text editor to create a file named `calendar` in your home directory. In it, type appointments, reminders, and snide remarks, along with the date on which you want them displayed. Here is a sample `calendar` file:

```
nov 5   Send invitations for Meg's birthday party
nov 20  Bought decorations for Meg's birthday party
        yet?
11/30   Get Meg a present!
12/4    Meg's birthday party at 11AM!
```

When you run the `calendar` program, it displays any lines that begin with today's date. To display calendar reminders every day when you log in, add this line to the end of your `.login` or `.profile` file:

```
calendar
```

When you log in on November 30, you see this message:

```
11/30  Get Meg a present!
```

# cancel

Cancels a print job (UNIX System V only). ***See*** the `lprm` command for BSD UNIX.

TIP

You can skip using `lpstat` if the job that you want to cancel is printing. Instead, you can specify just the name of the printer:

```
cancel lj
```

This line cancels whatever job is printing on the printer named `lj`.

## UNIXspeak

```
cancel requestID
```

| Option or Argument | Function |
|---|---|
| *requestID* | Specifies the print job that you want to cancel by using the request ID number listed by the `lpstat` command (which we describe later in this part). |

## Sample

To cancel the print job, you first find out its request ID by typing

```
lpstat
```

UNIX responds with a listing like this:

```
lj-1756      margyl     94832     Jan 12 10:43 on lj
lj-1762      margyl      1298     Jan 12 10:45 on lj
```

The first line describes the print job that you want to cancel (you can tell because its size, 94,832 characters, is big). Type

```
cancel lj-1756
```

UNIX responds

```
request "lj-1756" canceled
```

# cat

Displays a file on-screen.

`cat` only works with text files. For other types of files, you have to know which program created them.

If the file you want to look at is long, use the `more` command instead because it shows only a screen at a time.

TIP

You can also use the `cat` command (which stands for *catenate*) to combine two or more files, like this:

```
cat file1 file2 file3 > one.big.file
```

## UNIXspeak

```
cat filename
```

| *Option or Argument* | *Function* |
|---|---|
| *filename* | Specifies the name of the file that you want to see. |

## Sample

Type

```
cat bonus.plan
```

# cd

Changes the current working directory to the directory you indicate.

To move back to your home directory, type **cd** without any arguments.

To move to a directory that is not a subdirectory of the current working directory, you can use a full pathname — one that begins with a slash. For example, to look around in the `/home` directory (where all home directories are stored on some systems), type

```
cd /home
```

TIP

If you use the BASH or Korn shell, this command moves to the last directory you were in, as shown in the following line:

```
cd -
```

## UNIXspeak

```
cd [directory]
```

| Option or Argument | Function |
|---|---|
| *directory* | Specifies the directory you want to move to. This directory becomes your current working directory. If you don't use this option, you move to your home directory. |

### Sample

You log in and do some work in your home directory. Next, you want to move into your `budget` directory to see which files are there. Type

```
cd budget
```

Type **cd ..** to move back up to the parent directory of `budget`.

## chgrp

Changes the group that has access to a file or directory (System V only).

You have to own the file or directory to use this command. To change the group ownership of a bunch of files at the same time, you can use a wildcard in the filename.

If you use BSD UNIX, you can only change the group on files you own, and you can only change them to a group to which you belong.

### UNIXspeak

chgrp [-R] *newgroup filenames*

| Option or Argument | Function |
|---|---|
| -R | Tells `chmod` to change permissions on files in subdirectories, too. |
| *newgroup* | Specifies the name of the group that assumes ownership of the file(s). |
| *filenames* | Specifies the files you want to change. |

### Sample

You just created a form to be used by your organization's accounting department. To enable the department to use it, you want to change ownership of the file from your group to the `acctg` group. Type

```
chgrp acctg snazzy.form
```

# chmod

Changes the permissions for a file. You have to own the file or directory to use this command.

If you leave the who letter out of the permission, `chmod` assigns the permission to everyone.

Some people use numeric permission codes rather than the letter codes we favor. If someone tells you to set a file's permission to 440 or some other number, just ask for an English translation.

## UNIXspeak

```
chmod [-R] permissions filenames
```

| Option or Argument | Function |
|---|---|
| -R | Tells `chmod` to change permissions on files in subdirectories, too. |
| *permissions* | Specifies the permissions (also called the *mode*) to assign to the file(s). Permissions consist of a letter that tells who gets the permission, a character that indicates whether to add (+) or remove (-) the permission, and a letter that tells which kind of permission. |
| *filenames* | Specifies the file (or files) to change. |

| Code | Who Gets the Permission |
|---|---|
| u | User who owns the file |
| g | Group that owns the file |
| o | Other (everyone else) |
| a | All (everybody) |

| Code | Which Kind of Permission |
|---|---|
| r | Read the file. |
| w | Write or edit the file. |
| x | Execute (run) as a program (files), allow lookups (directories). |

## Sample

You created a shell script and now want to be able to execute it. Type

```
chmod a+x newscript
```

This line allows everyone to execute the script. To prevent others from reading it, type

```
chmod go-r newscript
```

# chown

Changes the owner of a file (System V only).

You have to own the file to be able to use this command. If you want to give a file to someone else, you may think that copying it to the person's home directory is enough. To give the person permission to use the file, however, it's best to change the file's ownership. After all, you can always keep a copy.

TIP: Another way to create a file with a different owner is for the new owner to copy the file. Helen can copy your report, for example. If she performs the `cp` command, she owns the copy. You just have to give her read permission for the file. (***See*** `chmod`.)

## UNIXspeak

`chown [-R]` *`newowner filenames`*

| Option or Argument | Function |
|---|---|
| -R | Tells `chown` to change the ownership of files in subdirectories, too. |
| *newowner* | Specifies the name of the new owner of the file (the current owner must be you or else the command doesn't work). Use the person's UNIX username. |
| *filenames* | Specifies the file (or files) to change. |

## Sample

You wrote a report and now want to pass it along to Andrew, who will finish it up. After moving the file to Andrew's home directory, type

```
chown andrew final.report
```

Now Andrew owns the file.

# clear

Clears the screen. This command doesn't affect files or jobs — it just clears the clutter from your screen.

### UNIXspeak

```
clear
```

### Sample

You just tried to use the `cat` command to look at a word processing document, and your screen is full of gibberish. Type **clear**.

## cmp

Compares two files and tells you the line numbers where they differ.

The problem with `cmp` is that it doesn't show you what's different about the files. For text files, you get far more information by using `diff`. On the other hand, `diff` cannot work with nontext files, and `cmp` can.

To compare three text files, ***see*** `diff3`.

### UNIXspeak

`cmp` *`onefile anotherfile`*

| *Option or Argument* | *Function* |
|---|---|
| *onefile* | Specifies the name of one of the files to compare. |
| *anotherfile* | Specifies the name of the other file to compare. |

### Sample

You have two versions of a letter you wrote, and you can't tell which is the final version. Type

```
cmp letter.to.dad letter.to.daddy
```

If UNIX says nothing, the two letters are exactly the same, character for character. Otherwise, UNIX tells you how far it got into the file before it found something different.

## compress

Shrinks a file into one "compressed" file so that it takes up less space on your disk.

When you want to get your original files back, you use `uncompress` or `zcat` (as we describe later in this part).

TIP: Compressing your files before transferring them over the network to another computer is a good idea. The smaller the file, the faster it transfers. If you want one big compressed file, create a combined file by using `tar` or `cpio` and compress the combined file.

## UNIXspeak

```
compress [-v] filenames
```

| *Option or Argument* | *Function* |
|---|---|
| -v | Displays how much the file(s) shrank. |
| *filenames* | Specifies the file(s) to compress. |

## Sample

You finished writing your magnum opus and mailed the manuscript to the publisher. You want to save all your manuscript files (named `chapter1`, `chapter2`, and so on) in a compressed format to save space. Type

```
compress -v chapter*
```

`compress` creates compressed files named `chapter1.Z`, `chapter2.Z`, and so on that contain freeze-dried versions of each chapter. It also deletes the original files.

***See also*** `gzip`, `gunzip`, `pack`, and `unpack`.

# cp

Copies one or more files.

If you know DOS, you may think that omitting the second filename tells `cp` to copy a file into the current working directory. This technique doesn't work in UNIX. Instead, use a period (.) to copy a file into the current directory.

WARNING: What happens if you copy a file to a new name and a file already has that name? Assuming that you have permission to write (change) the existing file, UNIX blows the existing file away and replaces it with the copied file. Always use the `ls` command to check that your new filename isn't already in use. And use the `-i` option to tell `cp` to ask before overwriting a file.

## UNIXspeak

```
cp [-i] oldfiles newfiles
```

or

```
cp [-i] [-R] oldfiles directory[/newfiles]
```

| *Option or Argument* | *Function* |
|---|---|
| -i | Asks before you replace an existing file with a copied file (only in System V Release 4 and BSD). |
| -R | When you copy a directory, also copies its subdirectories and creates new subdirectories as necessary. |
| *oldfiles* | Specifies the name of the file you want to copy. |
| *newfiles* | Specifies the name to give to the new copy. |
| *directory* | Specifies the name of the directory in which you want to store a copy. |

## Sample

You have a file that contains your January expense report. Rather than create your February expense report from scratch, you want to begin with a copy of the one for January. Type

```
cp january.expenses february.expenses
```

UNIX doesn't change the contents of `january.expenses` in any way — it just creates a new file called `february.expenses` with identical contents.

If you want to copy the `february.expenses` file from your boss' home directory, type

```
cp /home/harold/margys.feb.expenses
   february.expenses
```

By including both a path and a filename to copy to, you tell `cp` to copy the file from the `/home/harold/` directory and to name the new copy `february.expenses`.

# cpio

Adds and extracts files to and from *cpio format* archive files. Also copies files to and from things other than hard disks. Primarily useful for copying groups of files to backup tapes and for creating an archive file to be sent over a network.

## UNIXspeak

```
cpio -i [-c] [-d] [-E listname] [-u] [-v] [-V]
   [filenames]
```

or

```
cpio -o [-c] [-v] [-V]
```

or

```
cpio -p [-d] [-l] [-u] [-v] [-V] directory
```

| *Option or Argument* | *Function* |
|---|---|
| -c | Reads and writes archives in portable character format rather than in unportable binary format. |
| -d | Creates directories as needed; doesn't work with `-o`. |
| -E | Specifies that a file contains a list of filenames to be copied; doesn't work with `-o` or `-p`. |
| -i | Specifies that `cpio` extract the files from an archive back to the disk. |
| -l | Creates links to the files, if possible, instead of copying them; doesn't work with `-i` or `-o`. |
| -o | Specifies that `cpio` copy the files from the disk to an archive. |
| -p | Specifies that `cpio` copy the files from one directory to another on the disk. |
| -u | Copies files even if it means replacing existing files with the same names (watch out!); doesn't work with `-o`. |
| -v | Displays a list of filenames as it copies them. |
| -V | Displays a dot for each file that it copies so that you can tell how fast it's going. |
| *listname* | Specifies the name of a file that contains a list of files to copy; if you use this option, don't use *filenames.* |
| *filenames* | Specifies the names of the files to be copied; if you use this option, don't use *listname.* |
| *directory* | Specifies the name of the directory to copy the files to. |

TIP

To move a bunch of files from one directory to another, including all the subdirectories, you may be able to use the `cp -R` command. If this command doesn't work on your system, use the following magic incantation (it's ugly, but it's easier than any of the alternatives):

```
cd olddir
find * -print | cpio -pdlmv /usr/whatever/newdir
```

These commands move all the files from the `olddir` directory and its subdirectories to the `/usr/whatever/newdir` directory, creating new subdirectories as necessary. The process is rather like grafting a limb from one tree to another.

TIP

***Important note:*** Specify the name of the new directory as a full pathname. The new directory must already exist. (Use `mkdir` to create the directory if necessary.) After this command runs, the files exist in both the old and new directories — use `rm -r` to get rid of the old directory.

The `cpio` command is used also for copying files to and from tapes as part of a backup procedure. ***See also*** `tar`.

## Sample

You just finished a large project for which you created a bunch of files. You personally never want to see the files again, but you know that you should save them for posterity. To copy the files to an archive file, type

```
cpio -oc proj.plan report.draft report.final >
   proj.archive
```

This command creates an archive file named `proj.archive` that contains your project files.

Later, of course, it turns out that you have to make one or two little changes to your final report. To get the `report.final` file (and other files) back from the archive, type

```
cpio -icd < proj.archive
```

# crontab

Makes a list of programs that you want to run on a regular schedule.

## UNIXspeak

`crontab [-e] [-l] [-r] [`*`filename`*`]`

| *Option or Argument* | *Function* |
|---|---|
| -e | Edits your crontab file (usually with the `vi` editor by default). |
| -l | Lists the contents of your current crontab file. |
| -r | Removes your crontab file. |
| *filename* | Specifies the file that contains the list of commands and when you want to run each one. |

To use `crontab`, you need a *crontab file*. This file contains a list of commands that you want to run and the time and day when you want to run them. A crontab file is a text file, and each line of the file contains one command, like this:

*min hour DOM month DOW command*

The first five items specify when the command should be run, as described in this table:

| Item | Description |
|---|---|
| *min* | Minute (0 to 59) |
| *hour* | Hour (0 to 23) |
| *DOM* | Day of the month (1 to 31) |
| *month* | Month (1 to 12) |
| *DOW* | Day of the week (0 to 6, where 0 is Sunday) |
| *command* | Command to run |

You can use `crontab` only if your system administrator lets you. Your system administrator can also cancel commands that you have scheduled.

## Sample

You want to mail yourself a message every Friday to remind yourself to pick up groceries on the way home. You create a crontab file with the command `crontab -e` and then type this line into your crontab file:

```
0  0  *  *  5  echo "Pick up groceries!" | mail
   your username
```

This line indicates that at midnight (0 minute and 0 hour), regardless of the day of the month (*), in all months (*), on Fridays (day 5), you send a message to yourself by way of UNIX mail.

***See also*** `at`.

# csh

Runs the C shell, optionally running a script of stored commands.

The main reason that normal people run `csh` themselves is to run a script of C shell commands that someone else wrote. But because it's nearly impossible to write a C shell script that works, most scripts are written for BASH, the Bourne shell (`sh`), or the Korn shell (`ksh`).

### UNIXspeak

```
csh [script]
```

| Option or Argument | Function |
| --- | --- |
| *script* | Name of a file that contains a C shell script. |

### Sample

Someone gives you a C shell script named `new.program`. To run it, type

```
csh new.program
```

## date

Tells you the current date and time, taking into account your time zone and, if appropriate, daylight savings time.

### UNIXspeak

```
date
```

Far too many options let you control the exact format of the date display, but the one UNIX uses is usually clear enough. If you want to see only the date, for example, type

```
date +"%D"
```

If you want only the time, type

```
date +"%r"
```

TIP

True weenies stay up until 2 a.m. the first weekend in April and last weekend in October to make sure that the daylight savings time changes correctly.

### Sample

You wonder what time it is. Type

```
date
```

UNIX clears up any confusion you may have by displaying something like this:

```
Wed Sep 20 21:11:20 EDT
```

# df

Displays how much space on your disk is free.

## UNIXspeak

```
df [-k] [directory]
```

| Option or Argument | Function |
|---|---|
| -k | Displays only the amount of free space in kilobytes. |
| *directory* | Displays space on the file system where that directory resides. |

TIP

On System V, the directory name must be given as an absolute path starting with a slash. On BSD, any directory name will do.

The `df` listing includes lots of information about each *file system* (logical disk or disk partition) to which you have access, including its total size, the amount of space that's full (used), the free space, the percentage that's full (capacity), and, if it's a *network file system,* on which file server it is.

## Sample

You're wondering how much space is on the disk on which your home directory is stored. Assuming that your username is `elvis`, type

```
df /home/elvis
```

# diff

Compares two files and prints the lines in which the files differ.

## UNIXspeak

```
diff [-b] [-i] [-w] filename1 filename2
```

or

```
diff [-b] [-i] [-w] filename1 directory1
```

or

```
diff [-b] [-i] [-r] [-w] directory1 directory2
```

| *Option or Argument* | *Function* |
|---|---|
| -b | Treats groups of spaces (blanks) as single spaces, so it ignores spacing differences. |
| -i | Ignores the difference between uppercase and lowercase letters. |
| -r | When you're comparing two directories, specifies that subdirectories should be compared, too. |
| -w | Ignores all spaces and tabs. |
| *filename1* | Specifies one file to compare. |
| *filename2* | Specifies the other file to compare. |
| *directory1* | Specifies one directory to compare. If you tell `diff` to compare a file to a directory, it looks in the directory for a file of the same name and compares the two files (BSD only). |
| *directory2* | Specifies the other directory to compare. If you tell `diff` to compare two directories, it looks in both directories for files of the same name and compares all pairs of files with the same names. It also lists the names of files that are in one directory but not in the other. |

To compare two really big files, use `bdiff` instead. It works just like `diff`, only slower. To compare files that don't contain text, use `cmp`. ***See also*** `cmp`, `comm`, `diff3`, `dircmp`, and `sdiff`.

## Sample

You and a friend have been collaborating on a book (a purely hypothetical example). You both have copies of the various chapters in subdirectories of your home directories. The files should be exactly the same, but are they? To compare them, type

```
diff /home/margy/book /home/john/book
```

UNIX looks in the two directories and compares pairs of the files with the same names. For example, it compares the following files:

`/home/margy/book/chapter1` and `/home/john/book/chapter1`

`/home/margy/book/chapter2` and `/home/john/book/chapter2`

Whenever UNIX finds a difference, it prints the lines from both files, like this:

```
23c23
< was the largest chocolate cake she had ever seen.
—
> was the largest chocolate bar she had ever seen.
```

*(continued)*

*(continued)*

```
45a
> "More vanilla!" she said again.
62d
< The End
```

The report describes the differences by telling how to turn the first file into the second. `23c23` means that line 23 in the first file (it's listed beginning with a <) should be changed to line 23 in the second file (listed beginning with a >). `45a` indicates that a line should be added at the new line 45, and `62d` means that line 62 of the first file should be deleted.

# diff3

Compares three files.

## UNIXspeak

`diff3` *`filename1 filename2 filename3`*

| Option or Argument | Function |
|---|---|
| *filename1* | Specifies one file to compare. |
| *filename2* | Specifies another file to compare. |
| *filename3* | Specifies yet another file to compare. |

## Sample

You and two coworkers have proofed your committee's final report. You want to compare the changes made to the three versions. Type

```
diff3 report.margy report.john report.daveg
```

You see the differences in a format similar to that used by `diff`.

# dircmp

Compares two directories and tells you which files are in both, which are in just one, and which are in just the other. For files in both directories, the `dircmp` command tells you whether the contents of the files are the same.

## UNIXspeak

`dircmp [-d] [-s]` *`directory1 directory2`*

| Option or Argument | Function |
|---|---|
| -d | For files that are in both directories, compares them by using the `diff` command. |
| -s | Doesn't say anything about files that are identical. |
| *directory1* | Specifies one directory to compare. |
| *directory2* | Specifies the other directory to compare. |

The result of `dircmp` tells you only whether files are identical. ***See also*** `diff`, which can compare two directories and tell you exactly how files differ.

## Sample

Both you and your boss have been keeping copies of your department's monthly reports. Each of you has a directory named `Reports` that contains several files, and they seem to be more or less the same. You wonder whether either of you is missing any files and whether they all are exactly the same. Type

```
dircmp /home/margy/Reports /home/daveg/Reports
```

# du

Tells you how much disk space your files occupy.

## UNIXspeak

```
du [-a] [-s] directories
```

| Option or Argument | Function |
|---|---|
| -a | Displays the space used by each file, not just by each directory. |
| -s | Displays the total space used for each directory, but not subdirectories. |
| *directories* | Specifies the directory or directories to include in the disk usage listing. |

The size is usually reported in disk blocks, which are 512 characters or 1K characters, depending on your UNIX version.

## Sample

Your system administrator complains that your files take up too much space on the disk. "Nonsense," you reply, but then you realize that it may be better not to make her angry. Instead, you decide to refute the accusation with cold, hard evidence. Type

```
du /home/margy
```

You see

```
162    /home/margy/games
1492   /home/margy/book
5403   /home/margy/gossip
8550   /home/margy
```

# echo

Sends to its output, usually the console, whatever you type on the command line after `echo` and expands any wildcards by using *, ?, or `[ ]`.

## UNIXspeak

```
echo [-n] stuff
```

| Option or Argument | Function |
|---|---|
| -n | Doesn't begin a new line after echoing the information (BSD only). |
| *stuff* | Specifies the information to echo. If it is more than one word or contains punctuation, enclose the message in quotes. The section "Quoting Characters on the Command Line" in Part I contains information about including such special characters as carriage returns, tabs, and quotation marks themselves. |

## Sample

You're writing a shell script and want to display a message on-screen. In the shell script, include this line:

```
echo "Your report is now printing!"
```

When you run the shell script, this line displays

```
Your report is now printing!
```

# ed

Runs one of the world's ugliest line-oriented text editors. Part IV explains how to use `ed`.

# elm

Enables you to read and send mail. Part V explains how to use it.

# emacs

Runs a powerful screen-oriented text editor. Part IV explains how to use `emacs`.

# env

Shows you information about your UNIX environment variables.

## UNIXspeak

```
env
```

On some BSD systems, this command is called `printenv`. ***See also*** `set` and `setenv`.

## Sample

You're wondering which environment variables are defined for you, anyway. Type

```
env
```

You see a bunch of lines that look like this:

```
HOME=/home/margy
TZ=AST4ADT
```

# ex

A yucky, line-oriented text editor related to `ed` and `vi`. It's an extended version of `ed` (hence the name). For maximum confusion, you can also use `ex` commands within `vi`. Part IV explains how to use them all.

# exit

Logs you out. When you use `exit` in a terminal window, the window closes.

### UNIXspeak

```
exit
```

If typing **exit** doesn't work, try typing **logout**. Pressing Ctrl+D may also log you out.

When you use the X Window System, typing **exit** in the login window (the first window created when X starts up) not only closes the window but often logs you out.

### Sample

You finish working with UNIX and want to go home. Type **exit**. You see a message saying that you have logged out.

Or you're using a terminal window in X, and you're finished with it. To make it go away, type **exit**. The window closes.

## fg

Continues a stopped job by running it in the foreground. (Some versions of the Bourne and Korn shells cannot do this.)

### UNIXspeak

```
fg [%job]
```

| Option or Argument | Function |
|---|---|
| *%job* | Specifies the job number you want to run in the foreground. If you leave out the number, UNIX assumes that you mean the current job. |

Rather than use the job number from the `jobs` listing, you can use the first few letters of the program that's running. If the `find` program is running in the background, for example, you can move it to the foreground by typing

```
fg %find
```

### Sample

You're running a time-consuming program in the background by using the `bg` command (as we describe earlier in this part of the book). You decide to move it to the foreground because it's waiting for you to type something to it.

To check that the program is still running in the background, type

```
jobs
```

You see your job listed as job number 2. Type

```
fg %2
```

# file

Tells you whether something is a file, a directory, or something else entirely. If the thing is a file, the `file` command tries to guess which type of information it contains.

## UNIXspeak

```
file names
```

| Option or Argument | Function |
|---|---|
| *names* | Specifies the directories or files about which you want information. |

The `file` command can determine whether a file contains ASCII text. If it does, the `file` command can recognize certain types of ASCII text files, such as those that contain `troff` commands. It also recognizes compressed files created with the `compress` or `pack` programs. If `file` can't tell what a file contains, it suggests that the file is data. `file` uses some rules to guess what's in a file, so now and then it guesses wrong.

***See also*** `troff`, `compress`, and `pack`.

## Sample

You see an object named `Updates` in your home directory, and you wonder whether it is a file, a directory, or something else. Type

```
file Updates
```

You see something like this:

```
Update: directory
```

You wonder what's in the directory, so you type

```
file Updates/*
```

You see a list of the filenames in the directory with a guess about each file's contents.

# find

Finds one or more files, based on rules you give, and does something to them.

## UNIXspeak

```
find directories [-name filename] [-user username]
[-atime +days] [-mtime +days] [-print]
[-exec command {} \;] [-ok command {} \;]
```

| Option or Argument | Function |
|---|---|
| *directories* | Specifies a list of directories in which you want to begin the search. The find command searches all the subdirectories of these directories, too. If you want to start in the current directory, just type a single period (.). |
| -name *filename* | Specifies the name of the file (or files) you want to find. If you don't know the exact name, you can use the wildcard characters ? and *. A ? stands for any single character, and a * stands for a group of characters. You must quote the filename if you use wildcards. |
| -user *username* | Specifies the user who owns the files you want to find. |
| -atime +*days* | Specifies that you want only files that haven't been accessed (looked at) in at least *days* (the number of days). If you use a minus sign rather than a plus sign before the number of days, you get only files that were last looked at within that number of days. |
| -mtime +*days* | Specifies that you want only files that haven't been modified in at least *days* (the number of days). If you use a minus sign rather than a plus sign before the number of days, you get only files that were last changed within that number of days. |
| -print | Displays the names of files it finds. If you don't include this option, the `find` command may find lots of files, but it doesn't tell you about them. |
| -exec *command* {} \; | Runs *command* every time it finds a file. When it runs the command, it substitutes the name of the file it found for the `{}`. Be sure to type `\;` as a separate argument at the end of the command. |
| -ok *command* {} \; | Works the same way as the `-exec` option, except that it asks you to confirm that you want to perform the command as it finds each file. |

If you want to look in several places for a file, you can type several directories on the command line, like this:

```
find . /home/john -name chapter3 -print
```

This command looks in the current working directory (and all its subdirectories) as well as in /home/john (and all its subdirectories) for the file chapter3.

To search for a directory, use the -type d option, like this:

```
find . -name OldVersions -type d -print
```

This command searches for a directory named OldVersions.

To search for all the files you own (assuming that your username is stuart), type

```
find / -user stuart -print
```

This command begins the search at the root directory (/) of the entire file system, so it may take a while.

## Sample

You know that you made a file called business.plan, but you can't find it. Perhaps it's in the wrong subdirectory. In your home directory, type

```
find . -name business.plan -print
```

UNIX tells you that a file by that name is in your Planning directory, like this:

```
./Planning/business.plan
```

Or you want to print all files with filenames that begin with *recipe*. Type

```
find -name "recipe*" -exec lpr {} \;
```

As UNIX finds each file, it runs the lpr command to print it and substitutes the filename for the {} on the command line. Notice that you must enclose the filename in quotation marks if it contains wildcard characters.

What if you're asked to delete some files because your hard drive is running out of disk space? You decide to see whether you have files that you haven't looked at in at least three months (90 days). Type

```
find -atime +90 -print
```

Alternatively, you may want to see which files you've changed within the last week. Type

```
find -mtime -7 -print
```

# finger

Lists the people using your computer — with their real names, not just their UNIX usernames.

## UNIXspeak

`finger [`*username*`]`

or

`finger [`*@hostname*`]`

or

`finger [`*username@hostname*`]`

| *Option or Argument* | *Function* |
|---|---|
| *username* | Specifies the user (or users) about whom you want more information. |
| *hostname* | Specifies the hostname of the computer about which you want information. |

The `finger` command with no argument tells you who's using the computer you are using. The `finger` command with an argument gives you information about the user or system specified by the argument. If you're on the Internet, you can get information about any user on any system on the entire network. To find out who's on an Internet system named `mit.edu`, for example, type

```
finger @mit.edu
```

Some Internet systems respond with general information about the system rather than a list of who's logged on, and others let you search their user directories with `finger`. Other Internet systems consider the `finger` command a security risk and prevent the command from responding to remote machines.

***See also*** `who`.

## Sample

You wonder who else is using your computer. Type

```
finger
```

You see a listing of usernames, real names, and other miscellaneous information. You notice a username that you don't recognize, so you want more information. Type

```
finger andrewg
```

to get more information about the user *andrewg*. You see several lines about your friend Andrew Guertin, including his full name, his home directory, which shell he runs, when he logged in, which project he's working on (assuming that this information is stored in a file named `.project`) in his home directory, and his plans (from a file named `.plan` in his home directory).

You get some e-mail from *gillian@xuxa*. To find out who's on the `xuxa` system, type

```
finger @xuxa
```

The @ tells UNIX that this is the name of a system, not the name of a user. To find out more about the user, type

```
finger gillian@xuxa
```

# ftp

Transfers files from one computer to another over a network. Part VI explains how to use this command.

# grep

Finds lines in one or more files that contain a particular word or phrase.

## UNIXspeak

`grep [-i] [-l] [-n] [-v] text filenames`

| Option or Argument | Function |
|---|---|
| -i | Ignores case (uppercase and lowercase) when you're searching. |
| -l | Displays only the names of the files that contain the *text*, not the actual lines. |
| -n | Displays the line numbers of lines that contain the *text*. |
| -v | Specifies that you're looking for lines that *don't* contain the *text*. |

*(continued)*

| Option or Argument | Function |
|---|---|
| *text* | Specifies the word or phrase to search for. If the *text* includes spaces or punctuation that may confuse UNIX, enclose it in quotation marks. |
| *filenames* | Specifies the file(s) in which to search; to search all the files in the current directory, type * (asterisk). |

In addition to searching for plain text, `grep` can search for all kinds of patterns. In fact, `grep` stands for *g*lobal *r*egular *e*xpression and *p*rint, and it searches for *regular expressions.* Luckily, regular expressions look just like text, except for some punctuation that has special meaning to `grep`. The characters to watch out for are shown in the following table:

| Character | Meaning |
|---|---|
| . | Matches any single character. |
| * | Matches any number of the character that precedes it. For example, `.*` matches any number of any character. `X*` matches any number of Xs. |
| [] | Matches any one of the characters inside the brackets. For example, `[ABC]` matches one A, one B, or one C. `[A-Z]` matches any capital letter. |
| ^ | Represents the beginning of the line. For example, `^T` matches a T at the beginning of a line. |
| $ | Represents the end of the line. For example, `!$` matches an exclamation point at the end of a line. |
| \ | Tells `grep` to take the next character literally, not as a special character. If you want to search for I.B.M., for example, you can type `I\.B\.M\.` |

Related programs are `egrep` and `fgrep`. `egrep` is more powerful but more confusing, and `fgrep` is faster but more limited. For your sanity's sake, stick with `grep`.

## Sample

You're looking for the memo you wrote in which you mentioned microwaveable shelf-stable foods. To search all the files in the current directory, type

```
grep "microwaveable shelf-stable" *
```

You don't find the file you want. You realize that the M might be capitalized, so you tell `grep` to ignore capitalization by typing

```
grep -i "microwaveable shelf-stable" *
```

# gunzip

Restores a gzipped file to its normal size. The `gunzip` command also restores files compressed with `compress` or `pack`.

## UNIXspeak

```
gunzip [-c] [-f] [-r] [-v] filenames
```

| *Option or Argument* | *Function* |
|---|---|
| -c | Sends the uncompressed file to standard output (usually the screen) instead of to a new file; the original file is unchanged. (This is the same as using `zcat`.) |
| -f | Forces uncompression, even if a file with the same name already exists. |
| -r | Recursive; If any of the file names are directories, `gunzip` descends into the directory (and any of its subdirectories) and uncompresses all the files it finds there. |
| -v | Verbose; displays how much each file is being expanded. |
| *filenames* | Specifies the gzipped files to uncompress. |

TIP

If you want to see what's in the compressed file `facts`, type

```
gunzip -c facts
```

You see the uncompressed contents of the file on-screen, but no new file is created, and the gzipped file isn't deleted. You can use the `zcat` command to do the same thing.

To create a gzipped file, ***see*** `gzip`, later in this part. ***See also*** `compress`, `uncompress`, `pack`, and `unpack`.

## Sample

Someone gives you a compressed file called `facts.gz` that contains information you want. The `.gz` at the end confirms that this file is gzipped. Type

```
gunzip facts
```

(You can leave the `.gz` off the filename because `gunzip` assumes that all gzipped files have names that end with `.gz`.) `gunzip` creates a new file named `facts` that contains the information from `facts.gz`. It also deletes `facts.gz`.

# gzip

Compresses one or more files into one gzipped file so that it takes up less space on your disk. The compressed file has the same name as the original, but with the suffix `.gz` attached. When you want to get your original files back, you use `gunzip` or `gzip -d`. The `gzip` command does the same thing as the `compress` command, but `gzip` usually shrinks the files slightly smaller than `compress` does.

TIP

Compressing your files before transferring them over the network to another computer is a good idea. The smaller the file, the faster it transfers. If you want one big compressed file, create a combined file by using `tar` or `cpio` and then `gzip` the combined file.

## UNIXspeak

`gzip [-c] [-d] [-f] [-l] [-r] [-v]` *`filenames`*

| *Option or Argument* | *Function* |
|---|---|
| -c | Sends the gzipped file to standard output (usually the screen) instead of a new file; the original file is unchanged. |
| -d | Decompresses; the same as using `gunzip`. |
| -f | Forces compression, even if a gzipped file already exists. |
| -l | Displays how much the gzipped file(s) shrank. |
| -r | Recursive; if any of the file names are directories, gzip descends into the directory (and any of its subdirectories) and compresses all the files it finds there. |
| -v | Verbose; displays how much each file is being shrunk. |
| *filenames* | Specifies the file(s) to compress. |

***See also*** `compress`, `uncompress`, `pack`, and `unpack`.

## Sample

You have created a series of very large files and have put them inside a directory called My_Big_Files. Now you want to save all these files in a compressed format to save space. Type

```
gzip -rv My_Big_Files
```

`gzip` compresses all the files in the directory My_Big_Files and also those in any subdirectories it finds there. It also deletes the original files.

# head

Displays just the first few lines of a file (usually the first ten).

## UNIXspeak

```
head [-lines] filename
```

| Option or Argument | Function |
|---|---|
| *-lines* | Specifies the number of lines you want to see; if you omit this option, you get ten lines. |
| *filename* | Specifies the file you want to look at. |

TIP: On systems without a `head` command, you can get the same effect with the `sed` command. `sed` does all kinds of things (described later in this part of the book), but its `q` option displays lines at the beginning of a file. You can display the first 20 lines of the `master.plan` file, for example, like this:

```
sed 20q master.plan
```

## Sample

You wonder what's in a file called *master.plan,* but because it's very large, you want to see just the beginning. Type

```
head master.plan
```

You see the first ten lines of the file. You decide that you want to see more. To see the first 20 lines of the file, type

```
head -20 master.plan
```

You can also use `head` to see the first few lines of the output of another command. To see just the first 15 lines of the `man` page about the `ls` command, type

```
man ls | head -15
```

# help

If your UNIX system has an online help system, this command displays possibly helpful information about commands.

### UNIXspeak

```
help
```

### Sample

On some UNIX systems, you can type **help**. You see a little menu of topics, and you can display information about many UNIX commands.

Most UNIX systems, however, have no help system, and you see just an error message. It's worth a try, though. If you use BASH, it has its own help command that only tells you about BASH subcommands.

***See*** `man` to learn how to use the online reference manual.

## history

Lists the last 20 or so commands you typed. Works with only the C, BASH, and Korn shells.

### UNIXspeak

```
history
```

TIP

If you use the C or BASH shell, you don't have to type the command again. Instead, you can re-execute the last command you gave by typing

```
!!
```

If the command that you want is several commands back, you can still rerun it. To execute command number 5 in the History list, type

```
!5
```

If the command that you want is the most recent command you gave that begins with *gr,* you can type

```
!gr
```

If you use the Korn shell, you can also re-execute commands. To execute the last command again, type

```
r
```

To rerun the last `grep` command, type

```
r grep
```

If you use the Bourne shell, you're out of luck.

### Sample

You finally get a long, involved command to work (such as `grep` or `find`). A few minutes later, it disappears from the top of your screen (or terminal window). You want to give the command again. Type

```
history
```

You see a list of the last 20 or so commands, including the one you want to give again.

## id

Tells you what your numeric user and group IDs are and, on BSD, which groups you're in.

### UNIXspeak

```
id
```

### Sample

You want to know your user and group IDs so that you can tell your wizard what they are when you ask for help. Type

```
id
```

UNIX responds this way:

```
uid=275(johnl), group=50(staff)
```

## irc

Lets you access various Internet chat groups, which enable you to communicate "live" with other users connected to the Internet. Part VI explains how to use IRC.

## jobs

Lists the jobs that are running in either the foreground or the background or those that are stopped. (Some versions of the Bourne and Korn shells cannot do this.)

### UNIXspeak

```
jobs
```

After you list your jobs, you can move jobs to the foreground or the background — ***see*** `bg` and `fg`.

## Sample

Earlier in the day, you started a long, time-consuming job. To find out whether that job is still running, type

```
jobs
```

You see a list of all the jobs you're running in either the foreground or the background, as well as any stopped jobs. (You can stop the job in the foreground by pressing Ctrl+Z.)

# kill

Cancels a job that you don't want to continue.

## UNIXspeak

`kill %job`

or

`kill [-9] pid`

| *Option or Argument* | *Function* |
|---|---|
| *job* | Specifies the job that you want to kill. You can use the job number listed by the `jobs` command or a percent sign (%) and the first few letters of the program that's running (C and Korn shells only). |
| -9 | Tells `kill` to show no mercy in killing the program; kill it no matter what. Useful if milder measures failed. |
| *pid* | Specifies the process ID of the job. You can use the `ps` command to find out the job's process ID. (***See*** the `ps` section later in this part.) |

If a program is truly out of control, Ctrl+C may not stop it. In this case, you may have to find out its process ID *(pid)* to kill it. Use the `ps` command to see its pid (5246, for example) and then type

```
kill -9 5246
```

You can cancel only your own jobs, not jobs run by that ape in the next cubicle.

For a description of how to kill programs that don't want to die, see Chapters 13 and 24 of *UNIX For Dummies,* 4th Edition (IDG Books Worldwide, Inc.).

### Sample

You begin running a program called `big.report` and realize that you did something wrong. You stop the job by pressing Ctrl+Z; the message `Stopped` is displayed. To kill the program, type

```
kill %bi
```

Because `big.report` is the only program you're running that begins with the letters *bi,* that program dies.

## ksh

Runs the Korn shell.

The `ksh` command is most often useful when you want to run a Korn shell script that someone has given to you.

### UNIXspeak

```
ksh [script]
```

| *Option or Argument* | *Function* |
|---|---|
| *script* | Name of a file that contains a Korn shell script. |

### Sample

A friend gives you a Korn shell script named `fix.it.up` that you want to run. You run it by typing

```
ksh fix.it.up
```

## ln

Creates a new link to a file. Additional links can give a file more than one name or can make it live in more than one directory.

### UNIXspeak

```
ln [-n] [-s] existingfile newname
```

or

```
ln [-n] [-s] existingfiles directory
```

| Option or Argument | Function |
|---|---|
| -n | Tells `ln` not to clobber existing files when you're creating new links (a good idea). |
| -s | Tells `ln` to make a symbolic link to the file (not on older System V systems). |
| *existingfile* | Specifies the file to which you want to create a new link. |
| *newname* | Specifies the name to give to the new link. |
| *existingfiles* | Specifies the file(s) to which you want to create a new link(s). |
| *directory* | Specifies the directory in which you want the new link(s). |

A hard (non-symbolic) link to a file created by using the `ln` command works exactly the same way as the original filename for the file. You can use the `mv` command to rename the link, the `cp` command to copy the file, and the `rm` command to remove the link. (When you remove a link, the file may still remain. A file is deleted when its last link is removed.)

If you use files on other computers by way of NFS or some other system, you can't create regular links to those files — you see a message saying `ln: different file system`. Instead, you can create *soft* or *symbolic links* by using the `-s` option with the `ln` command, which acts as an alias for the file's original name.

If a file (or a link) already has the same name as the link you're creating, some versions of `ln` destroy the exiting file (or link) and create the new one. Using the `ls` command beforehand to check whether a file already has the name you plan to use is a good idea. Then use the `-n` option of the `ln` command so that it asks before clobbering existing files.

## Sample

You and your friend Katy both play backgammon, and she has a great new public domain backgammon game in the `bin` subdirectory of her home directory. Rather than make a copy of the program, which would waste space on the disk, you create a link to the file in Katy's directory. You move to your `bin` directory and type

```
ln /home/katy/bin/backgammon backg
```

Now the filename `backg` also appears in your `bin` directory, and it refers to the same file as `/home/katy/bin/backgammon`. If you want to create a link in the current directory by using the file's original name, you could have typed

```
ln /home/katy/bin/backgammon .
```

If you want to create links to all the files in Katy's directory, type

```
ln /home/katy/bin/* .
```

# lp

Prints a file (in UNIX System V only). For BSD systems, ***see*** `lpr` later in this part.

## UNIXspeak

```
lp [-c] [-d printer] [-m] [-n copies] [-o options]
   [-P pagenumbers] [-w] filename
```

| ***Option or Argument*** | ***Function*** |
|---|---|
| -c | Tells `lp` to make a copy of the file to be printed; if you edit the file between the time you give the `lp` command and the time it is printed, the changes don't appear in the printout. |
| -d *printer* | Specifies the printer on which you want the file printed. |
| -m | Tells `lp` to send you e-mail when the file has been printed; useful when the printer is busy and you may have to wait your turn. |
| -n *copies* | Specifies the number of copies of the file to print. |
| -o *options* | Specifies print options, listed below. |
| -P *pagenumbers* | Specifies which pages to print (that's a capital *P*). |
| -w | Displays a message on your screen as soon as the file has printed. |
| *filename* | Specifies the file you want to print. |

In response to the `lp` command, you see a message like this:

```
request id is lj-1024 (1 file)
```

The request ID number can be useful if you decide to cancel printing. (***See*** `cancel` earlier in this part.)

Suppose that you want to print your file on the high-quality printer in the executive suite and that the printer is named `execlaser`. Type

```
lp -d execlaser fin.info
```

TIP

If many people share one printer, a long delay can occur before your file is printed. If you want to see a message on-screen when the file prints, you can type

```
lp -w fin.info
```

Or `lp` can send you electronic mail after the file has been printed if you type

```
lp -m fin.info
```

If you want to print the output of another command, use redirection. To print a directory of files, for example, you can type

```
ls | lp
```

TIP

If you want to print several files, you can type several filenames:

```
lp fin.info memo4 letter.to.mom
```

Depending on the capabilities of your printer, you may be able to control the format of the output with the options in the following table, which you type right after the `-o` option:

| *Option* | *Description* |
|---|---|
| nobanner | Doesn't print a banner page (a page with your username and the name of the file). UNIX usually prints a banner page before each print job to separate one from the next. |
| nofilebreak | Doesn't start each file on a new page. |
| cpi=*pitch* | Prints the file at *pitch* characters per inch. Your printer may be capable of printing at a limited number of pitches, usually only 10 or 12. |
| lpi=*lines* | Prints the file at *lines* lines per inch (usually six). Some printers can print eight lines per inch. |
| length=*inches*i | Prints pages that are *inches* inches long. (Be sure to include the small *i* at the end of the option.) |
| length=*lines*l | Prints pages that are *lines* lines long. (Be sure to include the small *l*.) |
| width=*chars* | Prints a maximum of *chars* characters per line. |
| width=*inches*i | Prints pages that are a maximum of *inches* inches wide. |

To print several files with no page breaks between them, for example, you can type

```
lp -o nofilebreak fin*
```

### Sample

You create a text file that contains some important financial information that you want to pass along to your boss. Type

```
lp fin.info
```

After you print it, you decide that you want two more copies, so type

```
lp -n 2 fin.info
```

## lpq

Lists the status of available printers (in BSD UNIX only). ***See*** `lpstat` (in UNIX System V).

### UNIXspeak

`lpq [-P`*`printer`*`]`

| *Option or Argument* | *Function* |
|---|---|
| -P*printer* | Specifies the printer you want to know about; if you don't specify the printer, it assumes a default, usually the printer closest to you. |

### Sample

You have tried to print several large documents, but they have yet to appear on the printer. To look at the print queue for your printer, which is named *laser,* type

```
lpq -Plaser
```

UNIX responds

```
no entries
```

## lpr

Prints a file (in BSD UNIX only). For System V, ***see*** `lp` earlier in this part.

### UNIXspeak

`lpr [-P`*`printer`*`] [-#`*`copies`*`]` ***`filename`***

| Option or Argument | Function |
|---|---|
| -P*printer* | Specifies which printer to use. (There's no space after the -P.) |
| -#*copies* | Prints multiple copies of the file. |
| *filename* | Specifies the file you want to print. |

You can also print the output of another command. For example, this line shows how to print a `man` page:

```
man chmod | lpr
```

### Sample

To print a file named `status_report`, type

```
lpr status_report
```

If you decide to print it on a printer named `hplj`, type

```
lpr -Phplj status_report
```

## lprm

Cancels print jobs (BSD UNIX only).

### UNIXspeak

```
lprm [-Pprinter] [-] [job #]
```

| Option or Argument | Function |
|---|---|
| -P*printer* | Removes all the print jobs on the specified printer. |
| - | Removes all the print jobs owned by the user. |
| *job #* | Specifies the print job that you want to remove by using the job number listed by the `lpq` command (described earlier in this part). |

TIP

If you type **lprm** with no arguments or options, `lprm` removes the currently active print job if it is owned by you.

### Sample

To cancel a print job, first find out its job number by typing **lpq**. UNIX responds with a listing like this

```
lp is ready and printing
Rank    Owner   Job   Files            Total Size
```

```
active   daveg   275   some.file.txt   87,342 bytes
1st      daveg   276   other.file.txt  1753 bytes
```

The first line describes the print job that you want to cancel. (You can tell because its size, 87,342 characters, is big.) Type

```
lprm 275
```

UNIX responds with a message like

```
dfA275Aa02573 dequeued
cfA275Aa02573 dequeued
```

# lpstat

Lists the status of available printers (in UNIX System V only). *See* `lpq` (in BSD UNIX).

## UNIXspeak

**`lpstat`** `[-a] [-d] [-p` *`printers`*`]`

| *Option or Argument* | *Function* |
|---|---|
| -a | Lists all printers that are available. |
| -d | Lists your default printer (the printer on which your files print unless you specify otherwise). |
| -p *printers* | Displays the status of the printer(s) you name. |

To find all the printers on the network, type

```
lpstat -a
```

You see a list of printers, one per line, with the name and status of each one. If the printer is `accepting requests`, you can use it. To find out whether several print jobs are in the print queue for a particular printer — one named `execlaser`, for example — type

```
lpstat -p execlaser
```

## Sample

You send a large document to the printer, but then you change your mind. To find out its request ID, type

```
lpstat
```

You see a list of the print jobs waiting to be printed on your printer, including the request ID of each one. To cancel the job with request ID `hplj-78344`, type

```
cancel hplj-78344
```

# ls

Lists the files in a directory.

## UNIXspeak

ls [-a] [-l] [-p] [-r] [-R] [-t] [-x] [*pathname*]

| Option or Argument | Function |
|---|---|
| -a | Displays all the files and subdirectories, including hidden files (those with names that begin with a dot). |
| -l | Displays detailed information about each file and directory, including permissions, owners, size, and when the file was last modified. |
| -p | Displays a slash (/) at the end of each directory name to distinguish them from filenames. |
| -r | Displays files in reverse order. |
| -R | Includes the contents of all subdirectories, too. |
| -t | Displays files in order of modification time. |
| -x | Displays the filenames in columns across the screen. |
| *pathname* | Names the file or directory you want to list. |

If you want to see the sizes and modification dates of all your files, type

```
ls -al
```

You can combine several options together after one dash to save typing. This "long format" listing looks like this:

```
-rwxr-xr-x  2 mgmt john  14675 Nov 9  15:34 fin.info
-rw-rw-rw-  1 mgmt margy 3827  Nov 6  19:43 baked.beans
drw-rw-rw- 16 mgmt neil  128   Oct 1  11:31   Mail
```

This listing contains the following eight columns:

| *Column* | *Description* |
|---|---|
| Permissions | The first letter indicates whether the item is a file (`-`) or a directory (`d`). The remaining nine characters are in groups of three: The first group shows the owner's permissions, the second group shows the group's permissions, and the third group shows everyone else's permissions. Each group of three characters includes the read (`r` or `-`), write (`w` or `-`), and execute (`x` or `-`) permission. A dash indicates that the permission isn't granted. The permissions `-rwxr-xr`, for example, indicate that the item is a file (not a directory); its owner can read, write, and execute it; its group can read or execute it but not write on it; and everyone else can read it but not write or execute it. |
| Links | The number of names (hard links) that the file has. For directories, this sum is the number of subdirectories in the directory plus 2. |
| User owner | The name of the user who owns this file. |
| Group owner | The name of the group that owns this file. |
| Size | The size of the file in bytes (characters). |
| Mod. date | The date on which the file was last modified. |
| Mod. time | The time when the file was last modified. |
| Filename | The name of the file. |

Suppose the directory listing shows that you have a subdirectory named `bin` (the `bin` directory usually contains programs you use). To see what this subdirectory contains, type

```
ls -l bin
```

Suppose you're looking for all the filenames in subdirectories that begin with `bud`. Type

```
ls -R bud*
```

To list all the information about your files, sorted in reverse order of modification time, type

```
ls -ltr
```

If a directory listing is too long to fit on-screen, redirect its output to the `more` command so that you can see one page at a time, like this:

```
ls -al q* | more
```

Alternatively, you can list the filenames across the screen by typing this line:

```
ls -x
```

## Sample

You're working in your home directory and want to see a list of the files in it. Type

```
ls
```

But what about your hidden files, such as `.login` and `.profile`? To see information about all your files, type

```
ls -a
```

# lynx

A text-based program used to find and display information from the World Wide Web (WWW). Part VII explains how to use this program.

# mail

Lets you read and send mail. Part V explains how to use `mail`.

# man

Displays the reference manual page about a UNIX command.

## UNIXspeak

man [-] [-k *keywords*] ***topic***

| *Option or Argument* | *Function* |
|---|---|
| - | If your system usually presents manual pages one screen at a time, this option displays them without stopping — useful in redirecting the output of `man` to a file or to the printer. |
| -k *keywords* | Specifies one or more keywords to search for. You see all `man` pages that contain the keyword(s) in their header lines. |
| *topic* | Specifies the topic you want information about. The `man` pages are usually descriptions of UNIX commands, with a small number of general topics included, too. |

To print a manual page, type

```
man ls | lp
```

If you use BSD UNIX, redirect output to `lpr` instead.

If you use the X Window System, try running `xman` rather than `man`.

### Sample

You forgot the options that you can use with the `ls` command, so type

```
man ls
```

On some systems, the manual pages scroll right off the top of your screen. (Other systems automatically use `more` with `man` so that you see one screen at a time.) Type

```
man ls | more
```

To save this information for later perusal or inclusion in a user's manual you're writing for your department, type

```
man ls > ls.info
```

## mesg

Lets you control whether other people can use the `write` command to interrupt you with on-screen messages.

### UNIXspeak

```
mesg [n|y]
```

| *Option or Argument* | *Function* |
|---|---|
| n | Prevents messages from other users from popping up on your screen. |
| y | Allows messages to appear on your screen. |

Using electronic mail is preferable to using `write` when you want to communicate with other users.

### Sample

Another user is sending messages to you. The messages distract you and mess up your screen. Type

```
mesg n
```

Now, when users try to send messages, they see

```
Permission denied.
```

# mkdir

Creates a new directory.

## UNIXspeak

`mkdir directory`

| Option or Argument | Function |
|---|---|
| *directory* | Specifies the name of the new directory. If the name doesn't begin with a slash, the new directory is created as a subdirectory of the current working directory. If the name begins with a slash, the name defines the path from the root directory to the new directory. |

You must have permission to write in a directory to create a subdirectory in it. For the most part, you should create directories in your own home directory or subdirectories of it.

## Sample

You want a place to store some files temporarily. In your home directory, type

```
mkdir Temp
```

The next time you use the `ls` command, the `Temp` directory appears in your home directory.

# more

Displays information one screen at a time so that you can read it easily.

## UNIXspeak

`more [-s] [-u] [+linenum] [+/text] [filename]`

| Option or Argument | Function |
|---|---|
| -s | Squeezes out extra blank lines by displaying only one blank line. |
| -u | Ignores underscore and backspace characters, which can otherwise make text unreadable on-screen. |

| Option or Argument | Function |
|---|---|
| +*linenum* | Displays the file (or whatever the input to `more` is) as line *linenum*. |
| +/*text* | Begins displaying text two lines before the first time *text* appears. |
| *filename* | Specifies the file to display. |

When `more` pauses at the end of a screen, you can press any of the following keys:

| Key | Meaning |
|---|---|
| Spacebar | Displays the next screen of text. |
| Enter or Return | Displays the next line of text. |
| h | Displays help about what these keys mean. |
| q | Quits displaying this file. |
| / | Searches for some text. Type the text to search for immediately after the /, followed by Enter or Return. |

The `more` command is frequently used with redirection to display the output of another command. To see a long directory listing one screen at a time, for example, type

```
ls | more
```

## Sample

You receive a long memo in a text file. To display it on your screen, type

```
more long.memo
```

After displaying one screen of text, `more` pauses. Press the spacebar to see the next screen of text.

# mv

Renames a file or moves it from one directory to another.

## UNIXspeak

`mv [-i] `*`oldname newname`*

or

`mv [-i] `*`filename directory`*`[/`*`newname`*`]`

| Option or Argument | Function |
| --- | --- |
| -i | Tells mv to prompt you before it replaces an existing file with a moved or renamed file (works only in UNIX System V Release 4 and recent BSD systems). |
| *oldname* | Specifies the existing file you want to rename. |
| *newname* | Specifies the new name to use for the file. |
| *filename* | Specifies the file that you want to move. |
| *directory* | Specifies the directory to which you want to move the file. |

TIP

You can move and rename a file at the same time. For example, if you want to move your new.recipe file into your Recipes directory and rename it at the same time, type

```
mv new.recipe Recipes/veg.lasagne
```

You can also rename and move entire directories. Suppose that you want to rename your Recipes directory. Type

```
mv Recipes Food
```

The directory gets a new name. This operation doesn't affect the files in the directory.

Or suppose you want to move your Recipes directory and make it a subdirectory of your Personal directory. Type

```
mv Recipes Personal
```

WARNING

If another file already has the name you want to use, mv deletes it without telling you and replaces it with the renamed or moved file. To avoid this situation, use the -i option (for UNIX System V Release 4 and recent BSD system users only). Or use the ls command first to make sure that no file in the directory has the name you want to use.

## Sample

A coworker gives you a file named old.budget. You want to give it a better name, so type

```
mv old.budget 1998.budget
```

Then you decide to move it into your Budget directory. Type

```
mv 1998.budget Budget
```

# nice

Runs a command with lower priority so that the command doesn't hog the computer.

## UNIXspeak

`nice command [arguments] [&]`

| *Option or Argument* | *Function* |
|---|---|
| *command* | Specifies the command you want to run. |
| *arguments* | If you want to provide arguments for the command, type them just as you would if you weren't using the `nice` command. |
| & | Runs the command in the background; no one ever uses `nice` to run programs in the foreground. |

Many shells automatically `nice` anything that begins with `&`, so you may not have to.

## Sample

You usually run your monthly invoice report by typing

```
invoice.rpt 1999.12
```

except that you use different filenames for the argument. `1999.12` contains the data for one month.

The program slows down the computer, however, so you decide to run it in the background with low priority so that it takes longer but doesn't slow down the system so much. Type

```
nice invoice.rpt 1999.12 &
```

You see the process ID (pid) of the job and another prompt, so you can work in the foreground as the program runs in the background.

# nn

NETWORK

Lets you read messages posted to Usenet newsgroups. Part VIII explains how to use this command.

# pack

Shrinks a file into one *packed,* or compressed, file so that it takes up less space on your disk.

## UNIXspeak

```
pack filenames
```

| *Option or Argument* | *Function* |
|---|---|
| *filenames* | Specifies the files to compress. |

When you want to get your files back from a packed file, use `unpack` (as we describe later in this part of the book).

***See also*** `gzip`, `gunzip`, `compress`, and `uncompress`. The `gzip` and `compress` commands usually do a better job than `pack` does.

## Sample

You finish writing a large report and want to save it in a compressed format to save space. Type

```
pack long.report
```

`pack` makes a packed file named `long.report.z` that contains a shrunken version of the file and deletes the original file.

# passwd

Changes your password.

## UNIXspeak

```
passwd
```

The `passwd` command asks you to type your old password for verification and then type the new password twice to make sure you typed it correctly. None of the passwords appear on your screen.

You have to know your password to be able to change it. If you forget your password, ask your system administrator to give you a new one. Many versions of `passwd` try to enforce rules that require that the password be at least seven characters, contain digits, and otherwise be hard to remember. Often, if you try an unacceptable password three or four times, `passwd` gives up and accepts the unacceptable password.

## Sample

Type

`passwd`

UNIX prompts you for your current password to prove that you really are you. Then it asks you to enter a new password twice. Because the password doesn't appear on-screen, typing it twice ensures that no typo occurred when you typed it the first time.

# pico

Runs an easy-to-use, screen-oriented text editor. Part IV explains how to use this text editor.

# pine

NETWORK

Lets you read and send mail. Part V explains how to use `pine`.

# pr

Formats a text file with page numbers, line numbers, or other options so that the file looks nice when you print it.

## UNIXspeak

```
pr [-a] [-d] [-f] [-F] [-h text] [-l lines] [-m]
   [-n] [-o offset] [-t] [-w width] [+pagenum]
   [-columns] filenames
```

| *Option or Argument* | *Function* |
|---|---|
| -a | Prints lines across the page, in conjunction with *-columns*. This option is great when you have lots of short lines. |
| -d | Double-spaces the output. |
| -f | Uses form feed characters rather than blank lines to move to the top of a new page. (On some systems, this is `-F`.) |
| -h *text* | Prints *text* as the header at the top of each page. If you omit this option, `pr` prints a header that consists of the filename and the date the file was last changed. |

| Option or Argument | Function |
|---|---|
| -l *lines* | Sets the page length to *lines* lines. If you omit this option, the page length is 66 lines, which is correct when you're printing at six lines per inch on 11-inch paper. |
| -m | Merges several files together and prints each one in a separate column. |
| -n | Numbers the lines of the file. |
| -o *offset* | Prints *offset* extra spaces at the beginning of each line to make a wider left margin. This option is useful if you plan to punch holes in the paper or bind it. |
| -t | Suppresses printing of page headers or blank lines at the end of a file. |
| -w *width* | Sets the line width to *width* characters. If you leave out this option, the line width is 72 characters. This option is useful if you have a file with multiple columns. |
| +*pagenum* | Begins printing at page *pagenum.* |
| -*columns* | Prints the file in multiple columns, as in a newspaper. *Columns* is the desired number of columns. |
| *filenames* | Specifies the file (or files) you want to format for printing. |

To put line numbers at the beginning of each line, type

```
pr -n -h choco.story | lp
```

Later, after you modify the file, you want to print the original and new version side by side. Also, you want to add a one-inch (ten-character) left margin. Type

```
pr -o10 -m choco.story choco.story.new | lp
```

TIP

You can use `pr` only with text files, not with word-processing documents, PostScript output files, or other data files.

## Sample

To format a file named `choco.story`, type

```
pr choco.story | lp
```

This command formats the `choco.story` file and redirects the result to the `lp` command for printing. (If you use BSD UNIX, use the `lpr` command rather than `lp`.)

The last (fourth) page is smudged, so you reprint it by typing

```
pr +4 choco.story | lp
```

# ps

Displays information about your processes (jobs).

## UNIXspeak (BSD UNIX)

`ps [-a] [-l] [-ttty] [-u] [-x]`

| Option or Argument | Function |
|---|---|
| -a | Displays information about all processes. If you omit this option, you see only your processes. |
| -l | Displays a longer, more-detailed version. |
| -t*tty* | Displays a list of processes that were started by terminal *tty*. |
| -u | Displays a user-oriented report with additional information. |
| -x | Displays all processes that are running in the background and not using a terminal. |

## UNIXspeak (UNIX System V)

`ps [-a] [-e] [-f] [-tttys] [-u usernames]`

| Option or Argument | Function |
|---|---|
| -a | Includes information about almost all processes, not just processes you started. |
| -e | Displays all the processes in the entire system. |
| -f | Displays a full, more-detailed listing. |
| -t*ttys* | Displays a list of processes that were started by terminal(s) *ttys*. |
| -u *usernames* | Displays a list of processes that were started by the specified username(s). |

The `ps` command produces a listing with one process per line. Which columns you see depends on whether you use BSD UNIX or UNIX System V and which options you use.

| Column | Description |
|---|---|
| pid | Process ID, the unique number assigned to the process. You use the pid to kill the process if it gets out of control (***see*** `kill`, earlier in this part). |
| TTY or TT | Terminal ID where the process was run. |

| Column | Description |
|---|---|
| TIME | The number of minutes and seconds the process has run, counting only the time during which the process had the computer's full attention. |
| COMMAND or CMD | Command that began the process, more or less. |
| UID or USER | Username of the user who began the process. |
| PPID | PID of the process's *parent process* (the process that started this process). Sometimes, typing one command starts several processes. |
| C | Magic number related to how much CPU time the program has used lately. |
| STIME or STARTED | Start time (the time of day when the process began). If the process began more than 24 hours ago, this column shows the date. |
| STAT | Status of the process (`R` or `O` means that it's running right now). |
| %CPU | Percentage of the available central processing time the process has taken recently. |
| %MEM | Percentage of the available system memory the process has taken recently. |
| VSZ or SZ | Total memory size of the program, measured in kilobytes. |
| RSS | How much memory the process is using right now, measured in kilobytes. |

## Sample (BSD UNIX)

You wonder whether the process you ran in the background is still running. Type

```
ps
```

to see a list of all your processes. To see more information about them, type

```
ps -l
```

No option lets you see processes started by one particular user. Instead, you can use `grep` to find them. To see all the processes that were started by `lee`, type

```
ps -aux | grep lee
```

## Sample (UNIX System V)

You think that a program may be running amok, so type

```
ps
```

to see a list of all your processes. To see more information about them, type

```
ps -f
```

You want to check on your friend Lee's processes, too, so type

```
ps -u lee
```

# pwd

Displays the name of the current working directory.

## UNIXspeak

```
pwd
```

## Sample

You're lost and want to know which directory you're in (what the current working directory is). So type

```
pwd
```

You see a pathname like this:

```
/home/margy/Recipes
```

# rcp

NETWORK

Copies files to or from another computer (`rcp` stands for *r*emote *copy*). Part VI explains how to use this command.

# red

Runs a restricted (dumb) version of the line-oriented text editor `ed`. You can edit the files in only the current directory, and you cannot give shell commands. Even less useful than `ed`.

# rehash

Updates the table of UNIX commands and the programs they run (used only with the C shell).

## UNIXspeak

```
rehash
```

If you don't run rehash, UNIX can find your new program only when it's in the current directory. After you run rehash, it can find the program no matter what the current directory is. The program must be stored in a directory that's included in your PATH environment variable.

## Sample

You just wrote a shell script, which is stored in a file named do.it in your bin directory. To enable UNIX to find this new program when you type **do.it**, you update UNIX's command table by typing

```
rehash
```

# rlogin

Logs in to another computer (rlogin stands for remote login). ***See*** Part VI, which explains how to use it.

# rm

Deletes (removes) a file permanently.

## UNIXspeak

```
rm [-i] [-r] filenames
```

| *Option or Argument* | *Function* |
|---|---|
| -i | Asks you to confirm that you want to delete each file. |
| -r | Deletes an entire directory and the files it contains. Watch out — you can do a great deal of damage with this option! Always use the -i option. |
| *filenames* | Specifies the file(s) to delete. |

If other hard links (names) to the file exist, the file continues to exist. rm just deletes the name (link) you specify. A file actually dies when its last hard link (name) is deleted.

If you delete a file by mistake, talk to your system administrator immediately. If you're lucky, a backup copy of the file may be on tape. Unlike with some single-user systems, on UNIX you can't "undelete" a file.

### Sample

You made a test file, and now you're finished with it. Type

```
rm text.junk
```

The file disappears from your directory.

Suppose you want to delete all your old budget files. First, make sure that you know what you're planning to delete. Type

```
ls budget.93.*
```

If the list of files you see looks right, delete them:

```
rm budget.93.*
```

WARNING: Be extra careful when using wildcards like * together with `rm`; a simple misplaced space in front of the * causes the command to be interpreted as `rm *`, deleting all the files in the directory!

## rmdir

WARNING: Deletes (removes) a directory.

### UNIXspeak

`rmdir` *`directory`*

| Option or Argument | Function |
|---|---|
| *directory* | Specifies the directory you want to delete. (The directory must be empty already.) |

TIP: To delete a directory and all the files in it, you can use the `rm -ir` command (***see*** `rm`, earlier in this part). You cannot delete the current working directory, so move to its parent (by typing **cd ..**) before deleting a directory.

### Sample

After making backup copies of your files on a tape, you want to delete your `Budget` directory. First, you need to make sure that the directory doesn't contain anything you want to keep, so type

```
ls Budget
```

All the files listed are files you want to delete, so type

```
rm Budget/*
```

The Budget directory is now empty, so type

```
rmdir Budget
```

## rn

Lets you read messages posted to Usenet newsgroups. Part VIII explains how to use rn.

## rsh

Runs a command on another computer (rsh stands for remote shell). Part VI explains how to use it.

## script

Saves the conversation you're having with UNIX in a text file. (It stores everything you type and everything UNIX types back at you.) Works only with BSD UNIX and UNIX System V Release 4.

### UNIXspeak

script [-a] [*filename*]

| *Option or Argument* | *Function* |
|---|---|
| -a | If the file exists, it adds the new information to the end. |
| *filename* | Specifies the file in which to store the information. If you don't use this option, script stores the text in a file named typescript. |

If you're having trouble using the system, this command can be a useful way to document your input and the system's responses.

### Sample

You want to record your commands and UNIX's responses so that you can show your new trainee how to do something. Before giving the first command, type

```
script
```

Then give your usual series of commands. After you finish, type **exit** to leave script.

# sdiff

Compares two files by listing them side by side.

## UNIXspeak

`sdiff [-s] [-w width] filename1 filename2`

| Option or Argument | Function |
|---|---|
| -s | Suppresses printing of identical lines and prints only those that differ. |
| -w *width* | Specifies the width of your screen (use `-w 80`). |
| *filename1* | Specifies one file to compare. |
| *filename2* | Specifies the other file to compare. |

If the lines in the two files differ, UNIX puts a symbol in the column between the two files. If the line is in only the first file, the symbol is <; if it exists in only the second file, the symbol is >; and if the lines are different in the two files, the symbol is |.

***See also*** `cmp`, `comm`, `diff`, and `diff3`.

## Sample

Your boss makes some edits to your file. You want to know what those edits are, so you compare the edited version to your original by typing

```
sdiff memo4 memo4.original
```

# sed

Lets you use prerecorded commands to make changes to text (`sed` stands for stream editor).

## UNIXspeak

`sed [-f commandfile] [commands] filenames`

| Option or Argument | Function |
|---|---|
| -f *commandfile* | Specifies the file that contains the `sed` commands. |
| *commands* | Specifies `sed` commands to perform. If they contain spaces or punctuation, enclose the commands in quotes. |
| *filenames* | Specifies the file(s) that contains the original text. |

## Sample

You want to look at the first 20 lines of a file. The `q` command quits when it gets to the specified line, so type

```
sed 20q longfile
```

`sed` displays the file and quits after the 20th line. Or you can display the first 15 lines of output from the manual page about the `ls` command like this:

```
man ls | sed 15q
```

Or if you want to replace all instances of "Abel" with "Baker" in a text file, you can use the `s` command, like this:

```
sed "s/Abel/Baker/g" letter3 > letter3.new
```

This command reads the file `letter3`, changes "Abel" to "Baker" wherever it occurs, and stores the result in `letter3.new`.

***See*** Chapter 8 in *MORE UNIX For Dummies* (IDG Books Worldwide, Inc.) for more info about writing `sed` commands. The commands for `sed` are almost exactly the same as the ones for `ed`, which we describe in Part IV.

# set

Sets a shell variable to the value you specify or displays the value of the shell variable.

## UNIXspeak (Bourne, BASH, and Korn shells)

```
set
```

## UNIXspeak (C shell)

set [*variable* = *value*]

| *Option or Argument* | *Function* |
|---|---|
| *variable* | Specifies the variable whose value you want to set. |
| *value* | Specifies the value you want to assign to the variable. |

## UNIXspeak (any shell)

To see a list of the defined variables in your shell, type

```
set
```

To see the value of one variable, use the `echo` command like this:

```
echo $WORKDIR
```

UNIX forgets the variables you define when you log out. If you want to define a variable so that UNIX remembers it, add it to your `.login` or `.profile` file.

To get rid of a variable right away rather than wait until the next time you log out, use the `unset` command.

## Sample (Bourne, BASH, and Korn shells)

You want to set a shell variable to the name of a directory you frequently use. Type the following line (no spaces allowed):

```
WORKDIR=/home/fred/project/
```

Now you can use `WORKDIR` as the project directory name in your commands, like this:

```
cd $WORKDIR
```

In the Bourne and Korn shells, variable names are usually spelled with capital letters.

## Sample (C shell)

You want to set a shell variable to the name of a directory you frequently use. Type

```
set workdir=/home/fred/project/
```

Now you can use `workdir` as the project directory name in your commands, like this:

```
cd $workdir
```

In the C shell, variable names are usually spelled with small letters.

TIP: To set the value of an environment variable (a variable that's available to programs you run from the shell) in the C shell, you use the `setenv` command, as we describe later in this part. In the Bourne and Korn shells, type `export WORKDIR` to make `WORKDIR` an environment variable.

# setenv

Sets the value of an environment variable (C shell only).

## UNIXspeak

```
setenv [variable [value]]
```

| Option or Argument | Function |
|---|---|
| *variable* | Specifies the variable whose value you want to set. |
| *value* | Specifies the value you want to assign to the variable. If you leave it out, UNIX assigns nothing (the "null" value) to the variable. |

To see a list of your environment variables and their values, type

```
setenv
```

Notice that there's no equal sign in the `setenv` command, even though you have to use one with the `set` command.

## Sample

The PATH variable contains the list of directory pathnames that UNIX searches whenever you type the name of a program. Frequently-run programs should be stored in directories on the PATH list.

Suppose that you want to see your PATH list. Type

```
echo $PATH
```

Suppose that you have a `bin` subdirectory of your home directory and that it contains programs. You want to add this directory to your PATH list. Type

```
setenv PATH $PATH:/home/margy/bin
```

This line sets the PATH variable to its current value, followed by the pathname `/home/margy/bin` (substitute your username in place of `margy`).

# sh

Runs the Bourne shell.

## UNIXspeak

```
sh [script]
```

| Option or Argument | Function |
|---|---|
| *script* | Name of a file that contains a Bourne shell script. |

When you use UNIX, you're always using a shell. The other shells are the C shell (`csh`), BASH, and the Korn shell (`ksh`). You're likely to run `sh` yourself only to run a shell script that someone has given you.

TIP

If you receive a shar message by way of electronic mail, you run it as a shell script to create a file. A *shar message* is a sneaky way to send nontext files (short programs and shell scripts) through the mail. To recover the file from a shar message, save the message as a text file, use a text editor to remove all the lines from the beginning of the file up to the first line that begins with #, and then feed the file to the shell. If you save the shar message in a file called `shar.msg`, for example, you type

```
sh shar.msg
```

This command runs the script in the shar file and creates the program files that it contains. (A list of the files that the shar message creates is at the beginning of most shar messages.)

### Sample

A friend gives you a Bourne shell script named `check.all.files` that you want to run. You run it by typing

```
sh check.all.files
```

## sleep

Makes UNIX wait a little while, measured in seconds.

### UNIXspeak

```
sleep time
```

| Option or Argument | Function |
|---|---|
| *time* | Specifies the number of seconds to wait. |

You won't find much reason to use this command except in a shell script. If you want to execute a command at a particular time, ***see*** `at` and `crontab`.

### Sample

In a shell script, you want to pause before performing a command. You include this line in the shell script:

```
sleep 5
```

When you run the script, it pauses for five seconds when it executes the `sleep` command.

# sort

Sorts the lines in a text file.

## UNIXspeak

```
sort [-b] [-d] [-f] [-i] [-m] [-n] [-r] [-u]
   [+fields] [-o outputfile] filename
```

| Option or Argument | Function |
|---|---|
| -b | Ignores spaces at the beginning of a line. |
| -d | Uses dictionary sort order and ignores punctuation. |
| -f | Ignores capitalization while sorting. |
| -i | Ignores nonprinting control characters. |
| -m | Merges two or more input files into one sorted file. |
| -n | Sorts based on the number at the beginning of the line. With this option, 99 precedes 100 instead of following it, as it does in usual alphabetical order. |
| -r | Sorts in reverse order. You can combine this option with any other option. |
| -u | If the same line occurs in the file more than once, outputs it only once (stands for unique). |
| +*fields* | Considers each line to contain a series of fields (fields are separated by tab characters). When you're sorting, *fields* specifies the number of fields to skip from the left end of the line. For example, `sort +2` sorts beginning at the third field on each line. |
| -o *outputfile* | Specifies that `sort` should send the sorted output to a file and specifies the name of the file. |
| *filename* | Specifies the file that contains the text to be sorted. |

TIP

You can also sort the output of another command. For example, you can sort the list of lines that `grep` outputs, like this:

```
grep "eggplant parm" recipe.list | sort
```

The output of a number of commands (including `ls`) consists of fields separated by tabs, so you can sort it by using the `+fields` option. To sort a listing of files in numeric order by the fifth field (the file size), for example, type

```
ls -l | sort -n +5
```

### Sample

You want to sort a list of names into alphabetical order. Type

```
sort name.list > sorted.list
```

The sorted text is stored in a new file named `sorted.list`.

## spell

Looks through a text file and reports which words are not in the UNIX dictionary.

### UNIXspeak

`spell [-b] [+wordlist] filenames`

| Option or Argument | Function |
|---|---|
| -b | Uses British spellings. |
| +*wordlist* | Adds the contents of the file named *wordlist* to the UNIX dictionary so that words contained in the *wordlist* file are not considered to be misspelled. |
| *filenames* | Specifies the file (or files) to be spell-checked. |

`spell` works only with text files. If you use a word processor, use its built-in spell-checker instead. Also try running `ispell`, an interactive spell-checker that may be on your system.

### Sample

You use a text editor to write a memo, and you want to check your spelling. Type

```
spell memo.to.bob
```

Several words are rejected as misspelled. Then you remember that your friend Harold maintains a "jargon file" of nonstandard words that you frequently use. Type

```
spell +/home/harold/jargon memo.to.bob
```

Fewer words are seen as misspelled.

# stty

Sets the options for your terminal.

## UNIXspeak

```
stty [charname char] [sane] [[-]tostop] [-a]
```

| Option or Argument | Function |
|---|---|
| *charname* | Specifies the terminal control function you want to see. Refer to the following table to see what these characters are. |
| *char* | Specifies the key(s) that you want to use for this terminal control function. |
| sane | Returns your terminal to a "sane" state, which is useful if an editor dies and leaves your terminal in a state in which characters don't echo. |
| -tostop | Turns off terminal stop mode so that output from background jobs can be displayed on your screen. |
| tostop | Turns on terminal stop mode to prevent output from background jobs from being displayed on your screen. (Terminal stop mode is usually on, unless you have turned it off.) |
| -a | Displays all the terminal settings. |

You can change dozens of terminal settings, but you should leave most of them alone. The following table shows terminal control functions you may want to set.

| Name | Typical Character | Meaning |
|---|---|---|
| `erase` | Ctrl+H | Erases (backspaces over) the preceding character. |
| `kill` | Ctrl+U | Discards the line typed so far. |
| `eof` | Ctrl+D | Marks the end of input to a program. |
| `susp` | Ctrl+Z | Pauses the current program. |
| `intr` | Ctrl+C | Interrupts or kills the current program. |
| `quit` | Ctrl+\ | Kills the current program and writes a `core` file. |

To set your terminal options every time you log in, include your `stty` commands in your `.profile` or `.login` file.

### Sample

You want to use Ctrl+Q as the Backspace key on your terminal because you used it on your previous system. Type

```
stty erase '^q'
```

Be sure to put quotes around the key name so that `stty` and the shell don't get confused. The caret (^) means that you press the Ctrl key along with the letter, so `'^q'` means Ctrl+Q. If you want to specify the Delete key, use `'^?'`.

To list all your terminal settings, type

```
stty -a
```

## tail

Displays the last few lines of a file.

### UNIXspeak

```
tail [-r] [-lines] filename
```

| *Option or Argument* | *Function* |
|---|---|
| -r | Displays the lines in reverse order. |
| *-lines* | Specifies the number of lines you want to see (counting from the end of the file). |
| *filename* | Specifies the file you want to see the end of. |

Suppose you maintain a log file of changes to an important database. If you want to see the last 20 changes in reverse chronological order, type

```
tail -r -20 log.file
```

TIP

You can also use `tail` to see the last lines of output from another command. If you want to see the last ten changes Tonia made to the log file, for example, you can type

```
grep 'Tonia' log.file | tail
```

### Sample

You wonder whether you remembered to include a PS at the end of a memo you wrote. Type

```
tail memo.to.frank
```

You see the last ten lines of the file.

# talk

Lets you talk to another computer user by typing messages to each other on-screen.

## UNIXspeak

```
talk user[@computer]
```

| *Option or Argument* | *Function* |
|---|---|
| *user* | Specifies the username of the person with whom you want to chat. |
| *computer* | Specifies the name of the computer the person is logged in to. |

To talk to someone else on the network, try using the person's e-mail address as the computer name. If someone wants to talk to you but you don't want to talk back, you don't have to. To prevent people from talking to you at all, type **mesg n**.

## Sample

You use the `finger` command to determine that your friend Deb is logged on to the computer system in another building on your campus. According to `finger`, she's using a computer called `samba`. To chat with her, type

```
talk deb@samba
```

Deb sees a message on her screen like this:

```
Message from Talk_Daemon@iecc at 2:32 ...
talk: connection requested by margy@iecc
talk: respond with: talk margy@iecc
```

Deb wants to talk with you, so she types

```
talk margy@iecc
```

Now the top part of the screen shows what you type, and the bottom part shows what Deb types. (Deb sees the same thing, but vice versa.) Type messages to each other. After you finish, sign off by pressing Ctrl+D.

# tar

Copies a file to or from an archive file, backup tape, or floppy disk.

## UNIXspeak

```
tar c|r|t|u|x[v][w][0-9][f tarfile] filenames
```

| *Option or Argument* | *Function* |
|---|---|
| c | Creates a new archive file or tape, replacing any previous archive. |
| r | Copies files to the end of an existing file or tape. |
| t | Displays a list of all the files stored on the file or tape. |
| u | Copies files to the file or tape unless they're already there. If a previous version of a file is on the tape, tar copies the new version to the tape (tape only). |
| x | Copies (extracts) files from the archive file or tape. |
| v | Displays the names of the files as it copies them, plus `a` (for archive when you're copying to an archive file or tape) or `x` (for extract when you're copying from an archive file or tape). |
| w | Asks you to confirm the copying of each file. |
| 0-9 | A single digit says which unit to use. If you have only one tape or floppy, it's unit 0. Check with a local guru to find which value to use. |
| f *tarfile* | Specifies the name of the archive file. If the arch is on a disk or tape drive, the name is usually something like `/dev/fd096` or `/dev/tape`. |
| *filenames* | Specifies which files you want to copy. If you specify directory names, all files and subdirectories in the directories are included. |

Like disks, tapes can contain directories and subdirectories. You can extract all the files from a directory on a tape. To copy all the files from the `/Report` directory, for example, type

```
tar xvf /dev/tape /Report
```

The files are extracted into the current directory. If you use wildcard characters in the filename, be sure to enclose the entire thing in quotes, as shown in the following line, so that `tar` and the shell don't get confused:

```
tar xvf /dev/tape '/Report/*'
```

For information about making and using backups, see the section "Call in the backup squad" in Chapter 23 of *UNIX For Dummies,* 4th Edition (IDG Books Worldwide, Inc.).

## Sample

Someone gives you a tape and tells you that it contains a file you want. The file is called something like `mgmt.procedures`, and the tape drive is named `/dev/tape`. To find out which files are on the tape, type

```
tar tvf /dev/tape
```

You see that a file is named `manager.procedures`. Assuming that this is the file you want, copy it from the tape to the current working directory by typing

```
tar xvf /dev/tape manager.procedures
```

You can equally well use `tar` to create and unpack `tar`-format files, which are often used to pass around a bunch of files on networks. To put all the files in directory `project` in a `tar`-format file, type

```
tar cvf project.tar project
```

To extract the files from a `tar`-format archive, type

```
tar xvf project.tar
```

# tee

Copies text from a pipe into a file.

## UNIXspeak

`tee [-a] filenames`

| Option or Argument | Function |
|---|---|
| -a | Adds material to the end of the files if they already exist. |
| *filenames* | Specifies the file(s) to copy to. |

`tee` is most useful for making a log of the output of a slow-running or long-running program while still seeing its output on-screen.

## Sample

You're using the `find` command to find all your files that you haven't looked at for a month. You want to see the files on-screen as well as store the list of files in a new file named `stale.files`. Type

```
find . -atime +30 | tee stale.files
```

# telnet

NETWORK

Lets you log in to a remote computer. Part VI explains how to use `telnet`.

# time

NETWORK

Tells you how long a command took to run (from the time you pressed Enter or Return to the time you saw the next shell prompt).

## UNIXspeak

`time` *`command`* `[`*`arguments`*`]`

| *Option or Argument* | *Function* |
| --- | --- |
| *command* | Specifies the command or program you want to run. |
| *arguments* | Specifies the other information you have to type on the command line. |

In the C shell, `time` with no arguments gives the times (elapsed and the amount of the computer's CPU you have used) since the shell began.

The `timex` command works the same way, except that it provides options for which information you want to display.

## Sample

You're about to run your big monthly analysis report, and you're curious as to how long it takes to run. You usually type this command to run it:

```
agdata 1997-oct
```

Instead, use the `time` command to time it:

```
time agdata 1997-oct
```

After the report is finished running, you also see the elapsed time, execution time, and other information about how long the program took to run.

# tin

Lets you read messages posted to Usenet newsgroups. Part VIII explains how to use it.

# touch

Changes the date and time of a file without changing the file's contents.

## UNIXspeak

```
touch [-a] [-c] [-m] [-t date] filenames
```

| *Option or Argument* | *Function* |
|---|---|
| -a | Changes only the date and time the file was last accessed. |
| -c | Doesn't create files if they don't already exist. If you use `touch` without this option on a nonexistent filename, it creates an empty file. |
| -m | Changes only the date and time the file was last modified. |
| -t *date* | Specifies the date and time to give to the file(s). The date and time must be in the format *mmddhhnn,* where *mm* is the month number, *dd* is the day number, *hh* is the hour (using a 24-hour clock), and *nn* is the minute. |
| *filenames* | Specifies the file(s) whose date(s) and time(s) you want changed. |

If you leave out the date, `touch` changes the files' date and time to today, right now.

## Sample

You're about to distribute a bunch of files to everyone in your department. Because you may distribute updates later, you would find it convenient if all the files had exactly the same modification date and time (the date and time the files were last modified). All the files are stored in the `Distrib` directory. To set the date and time to noon on Christmas, type

```
touch 12251200 Distrib/*
```

# trn

Lets you read messages posted to Usenet newsgroups. Part VIII explains how to use it.

# troff

A baroque but powerful text formatter, `troff` uses a complex formatting language to format text files for output on a high-quality printer or typesetter. (`troff` stands for typeset runoff.)

## UNIXspeak

```
troff [-mmacrofile] [-nfirstpage] [-opagelist]
    filenames
```

| Option or Argument | Function |
|---|---|
| -m*macrofile* | Specifies the file that contains macros used in the input file. |
| -n*firstpage* | Uses *firstpage* as the page number of the first page that is printed. |
| -o*pagelist* | Specifies the pages you want to print (`3,6,15,21`, for example). |
| *filenames* | Specifies the file(s) that contains the input text. |

Suppose that the paper jammed when it printed page 8, so you have to print it again. Type

```
troff -o8 report6 | lp
```

When someone gives you a text file formatted for `troff`, the printing instructions may say to use a particular *macro file* that contains macros used by `troff`. If so, you may need to tell `troff` about the macro when you run it. If you're told to use the `ms` macros, type

```
troff -ms report6 | lp
```

If you want to find out how to format text for use with `troff` (or its predecessor, `nroff`), *UNIX in a Nutshell* by Daniel Gilly et al. (O'Reilly & Associates) gives a useful overview.

## Sample

Someone gives you a file that has been formatted for use with `troff` (that is, a text file that contains `troff` formatting codes, more properly called *requests* and *macros*). Luckily, you don't have to get into the world of `troff` formatting — you just have to print the file.

The file is called `report6`, and you usually use the `lp` command to print. Type

```
troff report6 | lp
```

# tty

Displays the device name of your terminal.

## UNIXspeak

```
tty
```

The terminal ID usually looks like the pathname of a subdirectory of the `/dev` directory. Actually, `/dev` is a directory (it stands for device) containing special files that are really connections to devices such as your terminal, printers, and tape drives.

TIP: In case something goes wrong, knowing your terminal ID is a good idea. If you have to ask your local UNIX guru for help, he or she will probably ask for the terminal ID. Try to sound as though you know what you're talking about; know your terminal ID.

## Sample

You need to know the name of your terminal so that you can report noise on the line to your system administrator. Type **tty**. You see

```
/dev/ttyd045
```

# umask

Tells UNIX which permissions to give to files and directories.

## UNIXspeak

umask [*permissions*]

| *Option or Argument* | *Function* |
|---|---|
| *permissions* | Specifies the permissions to give to files you create. Unfortunately, you must specify the permissions as an octal number by using the method described below. |

This table shows the numeric codes that make up a `umask` permission:

| *Number* | *Files You Create* | *Directories You Create* |
|---|---|---|
| 0 | Full access | Full access |
| 1 | Read and write | List files and create files |

| *Number* | *Files You Create* | *Directories You Create* |
|---|---|---|
| 2 | Read only | List and lookup files |
| 3 | Read only | List files |
| 4 | Write only | Create files and lookup files in directory |
| 5 | Write only | Create files |
| 6 | No access | Lookup files in directory |
| 7 | No access | No access |

A `umask` permission consists of three of these numbers: the first, your own permissions; the second, those for your group; and the third, for everyone else. The first number in your `umask` permission should always be 0 (zero) so that you give yourself complete permissions for everything you create. The most common umasks are 022, which enables anyone to read the files, but only you to write them; 002, to let members of your group change your files and others only read them; and 077, to let no one but you see any of your files.

TIP

You can always change the permissions for your files by using the `chmod` command, which we describe earlier in this part.

## Sample

Generally, when you create new files, you want everyone to be able to read the files, but you want only yourself and other members of your group to be able to write (edit) them. So you type

```
umask 002
```

When you create new files in the future, users who are not in your group can't edit the files.

# unalias

Removes an alias name (C, BASH, and Korn shells only).

## UNIXspeak

`unalias` *`names`*

| *Option or Argument* | *Function* |
|---|---|
| *names* | Name (or names) of the aliases you want to delete. |

***See*** `alias` for more information about aliases. If you use the Bourne shell, you're out of luck because aliases don't exist there.

### Sample

You created an alias for a directory you used frequently for a project. Now the project is over, and you don't want the alias anymore. Type

```
unalias projdir
```

Frequently aliases are set in `.profile` or `.cshrc`, in which case you'll have to edit the file to remove the alias command if you want to remove the alias permanently.

## uname

Tells you the name of the UNIX system you're using.

### UNIXspeak

```
uname [-s][-a]
```

| *Option or Argument* | *Function* |
|---|---|
| -s | Displays only the system name. If you don't use this option, you get a slew of other information. |
| -a | Displays all system name info. Without this option, you get just the local system name. |

To get the complete scoop about your system, type

```
uname
```

You see

```
plugh plugh 3.2.2 i386
```

You'll probably have to ask a UNIX wizard to decode this message for you because it contains version numbers, CPU types, and other technical information.

### Sample

You want to know the type of UNIX system you are using. Type

```
uname -s
```

You see the name of the system.

# uncompress

Restores a compressed file to its normal size.

## UNIXspeak

```
uncompress [-c] filenames
```

| Option or Argument | Function |
|---|---|
| -c | Displays the uncompressed version of the file but doesn't save it or delete the compressed file. |
| *filenames* | Specifies the compressed files to uncompress. |

TIP

If you want to see what's in the compressed file `facts`, type

```
uncompress -c facts
```

You see the uncompressed contents of the file on-screen, but no new file is created, and the compressed file isn't deleted. You can use the `zcat` command to do the same thing.

To create a compressed file, ***see*** `compress`, earlier in this part. ***See also*** `gzip`, `gunzip`, `pack`, and `unpack`.

## Sample

Someone gives you a compressed file called `facts.Z` that contains information you want. The `.Z` at the end confirms that this file is compressed. If a filename ends with `.z` instead, it is packed, and you must use the `unpack` command instead. Type

```
uncompress facts
```

(You can leave the `.Z` off the filename because `uncompress` assumes that all compressed files have names that end with `.Z`.) `uncompress` creates a new file named `facts` that contains the uncompressed information from `facts.Z`. It also deletes `facts.Z`.

# uniq

Removes repeated identical lines from a text file. If a file contains several adjacent lines that are the same, `uniq` deletes all but one.

## UNIXspeak

```
uniq [-c] [-d] [-u] [-f fields] [-s chars]
    [existingfile [newfile]]
```

| *Option or Argument* | *Function* |
|---|---|
| -c | Displays each line along with the number of times it occurs. |
| -d | Displays only lines that occur more than once. |
| -u | Displays only lines that occur only once. |
| -f *fields* | Skips the first *fields* fields on each line (fields are separated by either tabs or spaces) when you're comparing adjacent lines. |
| -s *chars* | Skips the first *chars* characters on each line when you're comparing adjacent lines. |
| *existingfile* | Specifies the file that contains the input text. |
| *newfile* | Specifies the name to use for the new file that contains the output; if not specified, sends output to the standard output. |

Suppose you have a text file named `visitors` that contains a list of the people who used your corporate library this month. The file contains one name per line, with the date preceding each name. You want to know how many times each person visited the library. Type

```
sort visitors | uniq -f 1 -c > name.list
```

This command line sorts the `visitors` file so that identical lines are together. Then it runs the `uniq` command: It skips the first field on each line (the date) and counts the instances of each name. It stashes the output in a file named `name.list`.

TIP

Unless your file is already sorted, you should almost always use `sort | uniq` rather than just `uniq`.

### Sample

You have an alphabetical list of the book titles in your corporate library, stored one per line, in a text file named `titles`. You think that some titles may have been entered twice. To get rid of possible duplicates, type

```
uniq titles titles2
```

## unpack

Restores a packed file to its original size.

### UNIXspeak

`unpack` *`filenames`*

| Option or Argument | Function |
|---|---|
| *filenames* | Specifies the packed files to unpack |

If you want to see what's in a packed file, you can use the `pcat` command to display its contents, like this:

```
pcat user.manual
```

You see the unpacked contents of the file on-screen, but no new file is created, and the packed file isn't deleted.

To create a packed file, see the `pack` command. ***See also*** `gzip`, `gunzip`, `compress`, and `uncompress`.

## Sample

Last year, you saved a file in packed format to save space. Now you want to use the file again. The file is called `user.manual.z`. The `.z` at the end confirms that this file is packed. If a filename ends with `.Z` (uppercase) instead, it is compressed, and you must use the `uncompress` command. Type

```
unpack user.manual.z
```

`unpack` creates a new file named `user.manual` that contains the unpacked information from `user.manual.z`. It also deletes `user.manual.z`.

# uucp

Copies a file to another computer by using the old `uucp` system.

## UNIXspeak

`uucp [-m] `*`yourfile computer`*`!`*`newfile`*

| Option or Argument | Function |
|---|---|
| -m | Sends mail to you after the file has been copied. |
| *yourfile* | Specifies the name of your file on your own computer. |
| *computer* | Specifies the computer to which you want to copy the file. |
| *newfile* | Specifies the name to use on the other computer when you're creating the file. |

You can specify where to store the file on the other computer, but `uucp` usually does not have permission to create files in any old directory. Instead, you may have to store it in `uucp`'s own directory, like this:

```
uucp big.news carioca!~/big.news
```

### Sample

You have a file named `big.news` that your friend is interested in. To send it to his computer, which is named `carioca`, type

```
uucp big.news carioca!big.news
```

`uucp` copies the file. If a transmission problem occurs, UNIX sends you electronic mail about it; otherwise, no news is good news.

WARNING: If you use the C shell, be sure to type a backslash (\) just before the exclamation point in the `uucp` command. Otherwise, the C shell interprets the exclamation point incorrectly.

## uudecode

Converts a uuencoded file back into its original form.

### UNIXspeak

```
uudecode [filename]
```

| *Option or Argument* | *Function* |
|---|---|
| *filename* | Specifies the name of the uuencoded file. If not given, reads from standard input. |

TIP: `uudecode` says nothing when it runs unless something went wrong. You have to look at the input file yourself to find out the name of the file that it decoded.

### Sample

A friend has sent you a uuencoded program by way of electronic mail. The message looks something like this:

```
begin 1746 run.me
LKJ3L409DFV13098D.V,,-F=0119208FH
""FLKJEO-19214309 ';'3;L46N-098ASD
```

By using your mail program (***see*** Part V of this book), you save the message as a text file named `uu.incoming`. Then you decode the file by typing

```
uudecode uu.incoming
```

uudecode decodes the file and creates a file named run.me. (The name to use for the decoded file is stored as part of the uuencoded file.) You delete uu.incoming, which you don't want anymore, and try running the run.me program.

# uuencode

Disguises a program as a text file so that you can send it through electronic mail or Usenet news.

## UNIXspeak

```
uuencode existingfile decodedname
```

| Option or Argument | Function |
|---|---|
| *existingfile* | Specifies the program (or other file) that you want to disguise as a text file. |
| *decodedname* | Specifies the name to be used later for the uudecoded file — after the file is mailed. |

## Sample

Your programming staff has written a fabulous new program that you want to share with a few friends. The program is currently called fish.squish, but when your friends receive it, you want it to be called run.me. Type

```
uuencode fish.squish run.me > file.to.send
```

uuencode creates a uuencoded file named file.to.send, in which the program has been transformed into a meaningless jumble of letters, numbers, and punctuation. You send the file to your friends via electronic mail. When they use uudecode (as we describe earlier in this part) on this file, it creates a file named run.me that contains the runnable program.

You can encode and mail your program in one fell swoop, like this:

```
uuencode fish.squish run.me | mail jordan@carioca
```

This command line uuencodes the file named *fish.squish* and mails it to your friend Jordan. When Jordan decodes the file, it'll be named *run.me*.

# vacation

Automatically responds to incoming e-mail messages by telling people that you're on vacation. (This command does not exist on all UNIX systems.)

## UNIXspeak

```
vacation [-l]
```

| Option or Argument | Function |
|---|---|
| -l | Stores the names of people who send you messages while you're away. The names are stored in a file named `.maillog` in your home directory. |

When you get back, cancel the `vacation` command by typing

```
mail -F ""
```

Doing so stops your mail from being forwarded to `vacation`.

## Sample

You're about to go on your annual two-week pilgrimage to Fiji, and you want people to know it. Type

```
vacation -m
```

Messages you receive are responded to automatically with a message saying that you're away on vacation. The wording of the response varies from one version of the `vacation` program to another.

# vi

Runs a powerful screen-oriented text editor. ***See*** Part IV to find out how to use it.

# wall

Displays a message on the screen of every single user on your computer network. Use with care!

## UNIXspeak

```
wall
```

TIP

Don't use this command except for important news of universal interest. Otherwise, you'll have angry officemates in a hurry.

Any user who turns off `write` messages with `mesg n` doesn't get `wall` messages either.

## Sample

Three shopping bags of Chinese food arrive in the reception area of your company. It's lunchtime! Type

```
wall
```

UNIX says nothing. Type this message:

```
The Chinese food has arrived! Come to the meeting
   room!
```

Press Ctrl+D to end the message. Your message is immediately displayed on every terminal.

# wc

Counts the number of lines, words, and characters in a file.

## UNIXspeak

```
wc [-c] [-l] [-w] [filename]
```

| *Option or Argument* | *Function* |
|---|---|
| -c | Displays only the number of characters in the file. |
| -l | Displays only the number of lines in the file. |
| -w | Displays only the number of words in the file. |
| *filename* | Specifies the name of the text file to count. |

## Sample

You spend two days working on an essay that's supposed to be no longer than 1,000 words. Type

```
wc my.essay
```

You see the number of characters, words, and lines in the file. If you want only the word count, type

```
wc -w my.essay
```

You can use `wc` to count the output of other commands. If you wonder, for example, how many files you have in your home directory and its subdirectories, you can type

```
find . -print | wc -l
```

This command finds all the files (beginning with the current directory) in the directory and its subdirectories. The output of the `find` command (the list of filenames) becomes the input to the `wc` command.

# who

Tells you who else is using this computer.

## UNIXspeak

```
who [-q] [am i]
```

| *Option or Argument* | *Function* |
|---|---|
| -q | Displays only usernames, not terminal IDs or other information. |
| am i | Displays your username, in case you have forgotten, or displays the username on any terminal that someone left logged in. |

The `users` command displays a list of the users who are currently logged in. On some systems, you can type `whoami` (no spaces) rather than `who am i` to find out your username. ***See also*** `finger` to get more information about who's on your computer or on the network.

## Sample

You wonder why your computer is so slow today. To find out who's using it, type

```
who
```

You see a list of usernames, terminal IDs, and login times.

# write

NETWORK

Displays a message on the screen of another user.

## UNIXspeak

```
write username [terminal]
```

| Option or Argument | Function |
|---|---|
| *username* | Specifies the person to whom you want to send a message. |
| *terminal* | Specifies the terminal the person is using. You have to mention this option only if the person is using several terminals (or terminal windows) at the same time. |

Sometimes `write` tells you something like this:

TIP

```
dave is logged on more than one place
You are connected to "vt01".
Other locations are:
ttyp1
ttyp0
```

Which terminal is Dave using? In reality, Dave is probably using only one terminal and is probably using several `xterm` windows under X Windows. Use the `finger` command to figure out which terminal is the one your friend is using.

***See also*** `talk` and `wall`. Better yet, use e-mail (***see*** Part V).

You can turn off `write` to the other user's screen by using the `mesg` command.

## Sample

You want to send an important message to your friend Dave, who works down the hall. Type

```
write dave
```

UNIX says nothing, so type the message and press Enter or Return at the end of each line:

```
Dave, it's Margy!
How about going out for some tacos?
```

At the end of the message, you press Ctrl+D. The message appears on Dave's screen.

# zcat

Displays the contents of a gzipped or compressed file on the screen.

## UNIXspeak

`zcat` *`filenames`*

| *Option or Argument* | *Function* |
|---|---|
| *filenames* | Specifies the compressed files you want to display. |

The `zcat` command does the same thing as `gunzip -c`. ***See also*** `gzip` and `gunzip`.

## Sample

You want to see the contents of a gzipped text file called `important.stuff.gz`. Type

```
zcat important.stuff.gz
```

Part III

# Using X Window Managers

*Window managers* are programs that control the way your screen is set up. They provide the border and buttons around a window, but are independent of what's inside the window. Several managers are used on UNIX systems. Motif and FVWM, which are based on the X Windows System, are the most popular, but others are still in use.

Only Motif and FVWM are described in this part. If you're stuck with a window manager other than these, ***see*** Chapter 4 of *UNIX For Dummies,* 4th Edition (IDG Books Worldwide, Inc.) for details.

## In this part . . .

- **Using the mouse to select and move stuff**
- **Opening, switching, moving, and resizing windows**
- **Doing mouse actions with keyboard shortcuts**
- **Exiting the window manager**

# Anatomy of a Window

Motif and FVWM windows look almost identical. Each window is surrounded by a border that contains lots of exciting pieces, as the following figure shows:

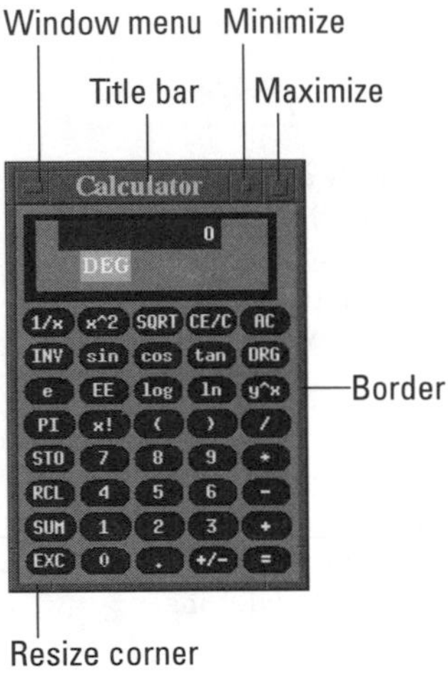


The following table explains what the parts of the window border do.

| *Name* | *Use* |
|---|---|
| Window menu | Displays the window menu. |
| Title bar | Moves the window. |
| Minimize | Turns the window into an icon. |
| Maximize | Makes the window fill the screen. |
| Resize corner | Changes the size of the window. |
| Border | Changes the size of the window (Motif) or moves the window (FVWM). |

# Changing the Window Size

You can change the size and shape of a window by using either the mouse or the keyboard.

With the mouse:

*1.* Move the mouse cursor to the window border. The mouse pointer changes to a little arrow pointing to a piece of border when you're in the right place.

*2.* Click and drag the border to make the window the size you want. In Motif, the side borders move left and right, the top and bottom borders move up and down, and the corners move in all four directions. In FVWM, only the corners change the window size.

Real mouse-haters use the keyboard:

*1.* Press Alt+F8 (in Motif) or Alt+F4 (in FVWM) to put the window in *resize mode.*

*2.* Press the arrow keys to change the window size. Holding down the Ctrl key while you press the arrow keys changes the size in larger increments.

*3.* Press Enter to accept the new size or press Esc to return to the old size.

# Exiting the Window Manager

Exiting the window manager returns you to the UNIX shell. Depending on how your version of Motif or FVWM is set up, you exit in one of two ways.

If you have a window called `login`, `shell`, `terminal`, or `xterm`:

*1.* Switch to that window. The window contains a UNIX shell.

*2.* Type **exit** or **logout** to exit the shell in that window, which tells the window manager you're done.

Otherwise:

*1.* Display the root menu by moving the mouse outside any window and pressing the right mouse button (Motif) or the left mouse button (FVWM).

*2.* Choose the command on the root menu called `Quit` or `Exit`.

WARNING: When you leave the window manager, it terminates every program running in every window without saving your work. Clean up before you exit.

# Keyboard Shortcuts

Keyboard shortcuts are the keyboard equivalents of mouse actions for the rodent-impaired who either don't have a mouse or don't want to use it.

Your system administrator can change any or all of the keyboard and mouse commands. If you try some of these shortcuts and something unexpected happens, ask your system administrator for details.

## Motif

| Key | Action |
|---|---|
| Alt+F1 | Brings the window to the front, on top of all other windows. |
| Alt+F3 | Drops the active window to the back, behind all other windows. |
| Alt+F4 | Closes the active window. |
| Alt+F5 | Restores an iconified window. |
| Alt+F6 | Switches to the next window. |
| Alt+F7 | Moves the active window. |
| Alt+F8 | Changes the size of the active window. |
| Alt+F9 | Minimizes the active window to an icon. |
| Alt+F10 | Maximizes the active window to fill the screen. |
| Shift+Esc | Displays the window menu (described later in this part). |
| Alt+spacebar | Displays the window menu. |
| Alt+Tab | Switches to the next window. |
| Alt+Shift+Tab | Switches to the preceding window. |

If you're familiar with Microsoft Windows, you'll notice that these key combinations are about the same as the ones Windows uses.

## FVWM

FVWM keyboard shortcuts are extremely customizable and are likely to vary from one computer to another. The shortcuts here are common default settings, but the ones on your computer may be different.

| Key | Action |
|---|---|
| Alt+F1 | Displays the window menu. |
| Alt+F2 | Displays the utilities menu (a list of applications). |

| *Key* | *Action* |
|---|---|
| Alt+F3 | Moves the active window. |
| Alt+F4 | Closes the active window. |
| Alt+F5 | Raises the active window to the front, in front of other windows. |
| Alt+F6 | Lowers the active window to the back, behind other windows. |
| Alt+Tab | Switches to the next window. |
| Alt+Shift+Tab | Switches to the preceding window. |

# Maximizing a Window

Maximizing a window means expanding it until it fills the entire screen. To maximize a window, do one of the following:

- ✦ Click the window's maximize button, the little block to the right of the minimize button.
- ✦ Choose Ma<u>x</u>imize from the window menu.
- ✦ Press Alt+F10 (in Motif or FVWM).

# Minimizing (Iconifying) a Window

When you minimize (or *iconify*) a window, you shrink it to an icon, which is a little box on-screen that represents the window. From the icon, you can *restore* the window to its original state, with any running program just where it was when you minimized it. You can minimize a window in one of three ways:

- ✦ Click the window's minimize button, the little dot near the upper right.
- ✦ Choose Mi<u>n</u>imize from the window menu.
- ✦ Press Alt+F9 (in Motif).

# Moving a Window

You can change the position of a window without changing its size. You can use the mouse, the keyboard, or both.

Using the mouse:

1. Move the mouse to the title area, the wide part of the top border that shows the name of the window. In FVWM, you can also move to either of the side borders or the bottom border.
2. Press and hold down the mouse button.
3. Drag the window to where you want it.
4. Release the button.

Using the keyboard:

1. Press Alt+F7 (in Motif) or Alt+F3 (in FVWM) to put the window in *move mode.*
2. Press the cursor keys to move the window. Holding down the Ctrl key while using the cursor keys moves the window in larger increments.
3. Press Enter to accept the new position or press Esc to return to the old place.

TIP

You can move a window off the edge of the screen if you want to get it out of the way for a minute.

# Opening a Window in an Obsolete but Easy Way

1. Switch to a window running the UNIX shell.
2. Type as a UNIX command the name of the program you want to run.

# Opening Windows in a User-Friendly Way

1. Move the mouse to a part of the screen outside any window.
2. Press the right mouse button (in Motif) or the left mouse button (in FVWM). If you have large windows, you may have to move one to clear some screen area. When you press the mouse button, a *root menu* appears. With luck, it has an entry for the menu you want.

You can, with some effort, customize your menus; see Chapter 19 of *MORE UNIX For Dummies.*

Several user-friendly shell programs also provide icons for popular programs; if you have one of these programs, click the appropriate icon.

# Restoring a Window

When you restore a window, you return it to its preceding size. To restore a window, do one of the following:

- ✦ Click the maximize button again.
- ✦ Choose Restore from the window menu.
- ✦ Press Alt+F5 (in Motif) or Alt+F10 (in FVWM).

# Restoring a Window from an Icon

You restore a window from an icon by expanding the icon back to the window that appeared before you iconized it. You must restore a window before you can use the program. Use one of these four ways:

- ✦ From the icon's window menu, choose Restore.
- ✦ Double-click the icon with the left mouse button.
- ✦ Single-click the icon with the middle mouse button (in FVWM).
- ✦ Move to the icon and press Alt+F5 (in Motif).

# Selecting Several Things with Your Mouse

You can select many items in an area, such as a chunk of text in a window.

1. Move the cursor to the beginning of the area you want to select.
2. Press and hold down the left mouse button.
3. While keeping the mouse button pressed, move the cursor to the end of what you want to select. The selected material changes color as you do this step.
4. Release the mouse button.

# Switching Windows

When you switch windows, you select which window is the *active* window, the window that receives text you type from the keyboard. Motif and FVWM make the border around the active window a different color from the others. Depending on your setup, you use one of these methods to switch windows:

✦ **Click-to-focus:** Move the mouse to the window you want and then click the mouse anywhere in that window.

✦ **Pointer-focus:** It's not standard Motif, but quite popular among FVWM users; you merely move the mouse to the window you want to use.

To tell which way you can select a window, move your mouse from one window to another without clicking. If the window borders change colors, you have pointer-focus. If not, you have click-to-focus.

You can bring any window to the front (that is, make it so that no other overlapping window obscures it) by clicking anywhere in the window's frame or by moving to the window and pressing Alt+F1 (in Motif) or Alt+F5 (in FVWM).

# The Window Menu

In the window menu, you perform standard window operations, such as changing the size of the window, moving the window, and minimizing the window to an icon. You can display the window menu in one of three ways:

✦ Click the little bar in the upper-left corner with the left mouse button.

✦ Click anywhere in the window border with the middle mouse button.

✦ Press Shift+Esc (in Motif) or Alt+spacebar.

The window menu is similar in Motif (left) and FVWM (right):

| | |
|---|---|
| <u>M</u>ove | |
| <u>R</u>esize | |
| Ra<u>i</u>se | |
| <u>L</u>ower | |
| (De)<u>I</u>conify | |
| (Un)<u>S</u>tick | |
| (Un)Ma<u>x</u>imize | |
| <u>D</u>elete | |
| <u>C</u>lose | |
| Destroy | |
| Scroll Bar | |
| Print | |
| Print Reverse | |

| | |
|---|---|
| Restore | Alt+F5 |
| Front | Alt+F1 |
| Move | Alt+F7 |
| Size | Alt+F8 |
| Minimize | Alt+F9 |
| Maximize | Alt+F10 |
| Lower | Alt+F3 |
| Close | Alt+F4 |

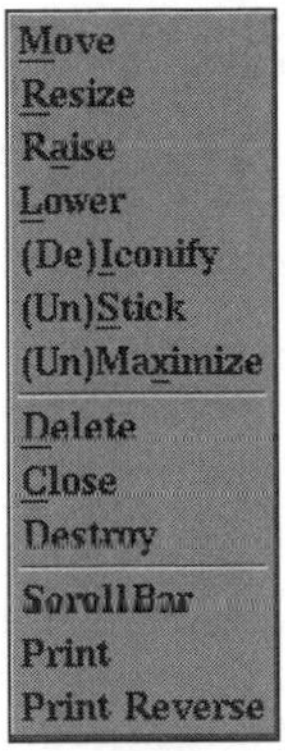

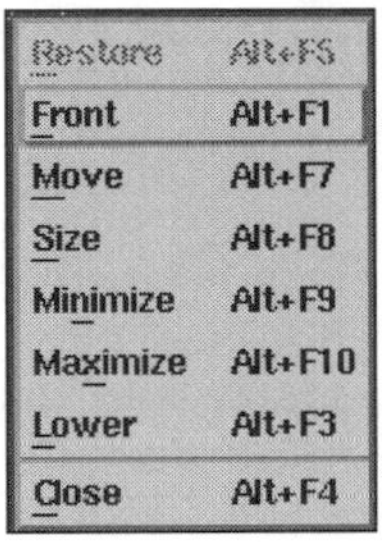

The window menu lists the most common window operations
along with their shortcut keys. Operations that aren't currently
valid are grayed out. You can select any of the menu entries in
three ways:

✦ Click the menu entry with the mouse.

✦ Type the underlined letter in the menu entry.

✦ Press the shortcut key combination (in Motif).

Icons (*see* the "Restoring a Window from an Icon" section, earlier
in this part) have window menus also, which you display in much
the same way: Click the icon with the left mouse button, click and
hold the middle mouse button, or press Shift+Esc or Alt+spacebar.

You can always use the shortcut key combination, regardless of
whether the window menu is displayed. If you do a great deal of
window wrangling, the shortcut keys are the easiest way to do
many window operations.

You can display the window menu and select an entry in one fell
swoop:

*1.* Move the cursor to the bar in the upper-left corner and press
and hold down the left mouse button.

*2.* When the menu appears, move the cursor to the entry you
want and release the button.

This menu, known as a *pull-down menu,* is used in lots of
applications.

# Working with the Common Desktop Environment (CDE)

The Common Desktop Environment (CDE) is an extension of plain ordinary X Windows. CDE looks just like Motif, but it also features a collection of GUI programs, a Front Panel from which you can run those programs (as well as any other UNIX applications), and drag-and-drop capabilities, so that many of the UNIX commands that we describe elsewhere in this book can be replaced by dragging icons around with your mouse. In keeping with its graphical, friendly, icon-based nature, the CDE refers to UNIX directories as *folders,* so that's what we call them here.

The CDE is standard with some UNIX systems, and available for many others.

## CDE Applications

The CDE comes with a suite of application programs that perform a lot of basic functions such as text editing, file management, and e-mail. The programs accessible from the Front Panel are

| *Program Name* | *Description* |
| --- | --- |
| Application Manager | A program that lets you start most commonly used UNIX programs by clicking a pretty icon instead of typing a command. |
| Calendar | A calendar/scheduler that lets you keep lists of appointments and things to do and gives reminders at the appropriate times. |
| File Manager | A program that displays files and directories as icons. Double-clicking an icon opens the file into the appropriate program. If the file is executable, double-clicking the icon runs it. Double-clicking a folder opens the directory. |
| Help Manager | A hypertext-based reference on how to use the CDE. |
| Mailer | A graphical mailer that lets you perform most mail operations with mouse clicks instead of with typed commands. |
| Printer Manager | Shows printer status and print jobs queued for all printers on the system. |
| Text Editor | A simple text editor like emacs, pico, or vi. Not as full-featured as those programs, but easy to use and fine for simple editing. |

## CDE Windows

Working with windows in the CDE is identical to working with Motif windows. The CDE window manager is called `dtwm` (for Desktop Window Manager), but its behavior and keyboard shortcuts are the same as previously described for Motif.

## The Front Panel

The predominant feature of the CDE that separates it from plain Motif is the Front Panel, with its drag-and-drop capabilities. The Front Panel appears across the bottom edge of your screen and is crammed full of clickable buttons.

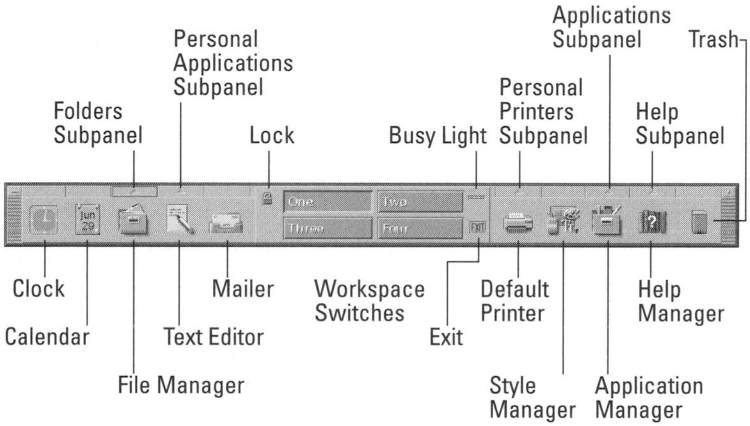


Here's what the various parts of the CDE Front Panel do when you click them:

| *Name* | *Action* |
|---|---|
| Clock | Displays the time. (This one is just a display – it's not clickable.) |
| Calendar | Starts the Calendar application. |
| File Manager | Starts the File Manager in your home folder. |
| Text Editor | Starts a simple text editor. |
| Mailer | Starts the Mailer, a graphical mail program. |
| Lock | Locks the workstation so that others can't use it while you're away. Unlock it with your password. |

*(continued)*

| Name | Action |
|---|---|
| Workspace | Switch between workspaces. Each workspace is like a separate desktop with its own windows in it. CDE lets you have up to four workspaces, which you can switch between by clicking these buttons. |
| Busy Light | Shows system activity. |
| Exit | Logs out. |
| Printer | Shows print jobs queued for the default printer. |
| Style Manager | Changes the appearance of your desktop (window colors, backdrop patterns, fonts, sounds, and so on). |
| Application Manager | Starts the Application Manager. |
| Help | Starts the Help Manager. |
| Trash | Shows the contents of the trash can. |

Some of the Front Panel buttons let you drag and drop icons on them. Here's what happens when you drag an icon from the File Manager and drop it on these buttons:

| Button | Action on Dropped File or Folder |
|---|---|
| File Manager | Opens a dropped folder in the File Manager. |
| Text Editor | Opens a dropped file in the Text Editor. |
| Mailer | Opens a dropped file in the Mailer's compose window. |
| Printer | Prints a dropped file on the default printer. |
| Trash | Moves a dropped file or folder to the trash can. |

## Front Panel Subpanels

Five of the Front Panel icons have small triangles above them. Clicking the small triangle pops up a subpanel, which is a small set of clickable menu items. Components of the five subpanels are listed below:

| Subpanel Name | Description |
|---|---|
| Applications | In addition to an icon for the Application Manager, this subpanel has shortcuts to subgroups of applications, such as Desktop_Apps and Desktop_Controls. |
| Help | In addition to the Help Manager, this subpanel has shortcut icons for help on specific topics, such as the Front Panel and the Desktop. |

| *Subpanel Name* | *Description* |
|---|---|
| Folders | A list of folders to open into the file manager. In addition to your home folder, this subpanel has options for floppy disk, CD-ROM, and personal bookmarks. You can also add other folders with the Install Icon control. |
| Personal Applications | Like the Applications subpanel, except that it is a short, configurable list that you set up for applications that you use most often. |
| Personal Printers | Opens the Print Manager for any installed printer, not just the default printer. |

TIP

The menu item that is at the top of the subpanel is the one that you get by clicking the Front Panel icon.

You can configure a subpanel to your liking by adding icons with the Install Icon control. To add an application to the Front Panel, drag its icon from the Application Manager to Install Icon, and it will be copied to the subpanel. You can also drag data files and folders to the Install Icon control.

# Part IV

## Using Text Editors (ed, emacs, pico, and vi)

Text editors let you write and save text files, such as shell scripts, e-mail messages, programs, and configuration files such as your `.login` or `.profile` files.

Text editors do not have the advanced formatting functions that you find in word processors. However, you can easily read files created with these programs and send files created with text editors over a network.

### In this part . . .

- **Using `ed`, an old-fashioned, simple line editor**
- **Using `emacs`, a powerful, full-featured, screen-based editor**
- **Using `pico`, an easy-to-use screen-based editor**
- **Using `vi`, a popular screen-based editor found on almost all systems**

# Using the ed Text Editor

ed is an old-fashioned line-at-a-time editor that's used to edit text files, such as electronic-mail messages or shell scripts. Line editors like ed made a lot of sense back in the days of teletypes and rolls of paper. Because screen editors — which let you see and edit files a screen at a time — are much easier to use (***see*** emacs, pico, and vi later in this part), use ed only if other editors are not available on your system.

## Starting ed

To start ed, simply type **ed** at the shell prompt.

To create a new file and give it a name or to load an existing file, type

```
ed filename
```

If the file already exists, you see the number of characters in it. If you're creating a new file, you see a question mark.

To complicate matters, ed is always in either *command mode* or *input mode*. In command mode, letters you type are interpreted as commands. In input mode, what you type is entered in the file you're editing.

TIP: To make ed more usable, press P to put it into *prompt mode* so that it displays an asterisk whenever it is in command mode and waiting for a command. Then press H to tell ed to display more helpful messages when something goes wrong.

## Getting out of ed

1. If you're in input mode, type a period and press Enter to go to command mode.
2. Press w to save your work (unless you don't want to).
3. Press q to quit the program. You see the shell prompt again.

If you want to exit ed without saving the changes you made to the file, press q. When ed displays a question mark, press q again.

## ed commands

All ed commands consist of one letter. Be sure to use the same capitalization shown in this section — most basic ed commands are lowercase.

ed commands work with one line at a time. The line you're presently using is called the *current line*, and commands apply to that line unless you say otherwise.

| *Command* | *What It Does* |
|---|---|
| a | Appends text (that is, adds a line after the current line and switches to input mode). To exit input mode and return to command mode, type a period on a line by itself. |
| *n*a | Appends text after line number *n*. |
| d | Deletes current line. |
| *n*d | Deletes line number *n*. |
| *n,m*d | Deletes lines numbered *n* through *m*. |
| h | Displays an explanation of the most recent error, if any. |
| H | Displays help messages whenever anything goes wrong. |
| i | Inserts text (that is, inserts a line before the current line and switches to input mode). To exit input mode and return to command mode, type a period on a line by itself. |
| *n*i | Inserts text before line number *n*. |
| n | Displays the current line with a line number. |
| *n,m*n | Displays lines numbered *n* through *m* with line numbers. |
| 1,$n | Displays all the lines in the file with line numbers. |
| p | Displays the current line without line numbers. (We recommend using the n command instead because you have to know line numbers to edit the lines.) |
| *n,m*p | Displays lines numbered *n* through *m* without line numbers. |
| 1,$p | Displays all the lines in the file without line numbers. |
| P | Displays an asterisk whenever ed is in command mode. |
| q | Quits the program. |
| Q | Quits even if changes haven't been saved. |
| s/*text1*/*text2*/ | Substitutes *text2* for *text1* the first place it appears in the current line. |
| *n,m*s/*text1*/*text2*/ | Substitutes *text2* for *text1* the first place it appears in each line numbered *n* through *m*. |
| u | Undoes the last change you made. |
| w | Writes (saves) the file. |
| Enter (or Return) | Displays the next line of the file. |
| . (period) | Displays the next line of the file. In input mode, typing a period on a line by itself returns you to command mode. |

There are lots of other ed commands — almost every letter is a command. Be careful what you type while you're in command mode!

***See also*** *UNIX For Dummies,* 4th Edition, Chapter 10, and *MORE UNIX For Dummies,* Chapters 11 and 12, for more information about `ed`, `emacs`, `pico`, and `vi`.

# Using the emacs Text Editor

`emacs` is a powerful screen editor that enables you to edit multiple files at one time.

## Starting emacs

To start `emacs`, simply type **emacs**. To create a new file and give it a name or to load an existing file, at the shell prompt type

```
emacs filename
```

`emacs` displays the first screen of the file. The cursor is at the beginning of the file.

On some systems, the `emacs` program is named `e` or `gmacs` or `epsilon`. Some UNIX installations don't have `emacs`. (But they should.)

## Getting out of emacs

1. Save your work by pressing Ctrl+x, Ctrl+s.
2. Exit `emacs` by pressing Ctrl+x, Ctrl+c. You see the shell prompt.

## emacs commands

You type commands by using various combinations of the Ctrl and Meta keys. Unfortunately, your keyboard probably does not have a key marked Meta, so press the Alt key instead. If you don't have an Alt key or your Alt key doesn't work with UNIX, press the Esc key and then the key that it modifies. (If you use Esc for Meta, you need to let go of the Esc key before pressing the next key.)

| *Command* | *What It Does* |
|---|---|
| Meta+< (that is, Meta+Shift+comma) | Moves the cursor to the beginning of the file. |
| Meta+> | Moves the cursor to the end of the file. |
| Meta+% | Replaces all occurrences of one piece of text with another. `emacs` asks you for the text to be replaced and the text to replace it with. |

| *Command* | *What It Does* |
|---|---|
| Ctrl+@ (that is, Ctrl+Shift+2) | Puts a *mark* at the cursor location. After you move the cursor, you can move or copy the text between the mark and the cursor by using the Ctrl+w or Meta+w keystroke. |
| Ctrl+a | Moves the cursor to the beginning of the line. |
| Ctrl+b | Moves the cursor back one character. |
| Meta+b | Moves the cursor back one word. |
| Ctrl+d | Deletes the character under the cursor. |
| Meta+d | Deletes the current word. |
| Ctrl+e | Moves the cursor to the end of the line. |
| Ctrl+f | Moves the cursor forward one character. |
| Meta+f | Moves the cursor forward one word. |
| Ctrl+g | Cancels the current command. |
| Ctrl+h | Enters the online help system. |
| Ctrl+h c | Displays the command that runs when you press a particular key. |
| Ctrl+h t | Runs a tutorial about `emacs`. |
| Ctrl+k | Deletes ("kills") the text from the cursor to the end of the line and stores it in the *kill buffer.* |
| Ctrl+n | Moves the cursor to the next line. |
| Ctrl+p | Moves the cursor to the preceding line. |
| Meta+q | Reformats the current paragraph by using word wrap so that the lines are full. |
| Ctrl+s | Searches for text. When you find what you're looking for, press Esc or move the cursor. To repeat the search, press Ctrl+s again. |
| Meta+s | Centers the current line. |
| Ctrl+t | Transposes the characters before and under the cursor. |
| Meta+t | Transposes the two words before the cursor. |
| Meta+u | Capitalizes the current word from the cursor to the end of the word. |
| Meta+l | Lowercases the current word from the cursor to the end of the word. |
| Meta+c | Capitalizes the letter under the cursor; lowercases the rest of the letters to the end of the word. |
| Ctrl+v | Scrolls down one screen. |
| Meta+v | Scrolls up one screen. |

*(continued)*

| Command | What It Does |
|---|---|
| Ctrl+w | Deletes ("whomps") the text between the mark (set by using Ctrl+@) and the cursor and stores it in the kill buffer. To get it back, press Ctrl+y. |
| Meta+w | Copies the text between the mark and the cursor to the kill buffer so that you can insert copies of it by using Ctrl+y. |
| Ctrl+x Ctrl+c | Exits `emacs`. |
| Ctrl+x Ctrl+s | Saves the file. |
| Ctrl+x Ctrl+u | Undoes the last change. |
| Meta+x doctor (followed by Enter) | Stops doing useful work and starts "doctor mode," playing a game in which `emacs` responds to your statements with questions. Save your work first. Not all versions of `emacs` support this mode. |
| Ctrl+y | Inserts ("yanks") the text that is in the kill buffer and places it after the cursor. |
| Del (the Del key) | Deletes the character under the cursor. |
| Meta+Del | Deletes the word in front of the cursor. |

## emacs commands for editing multiple files

You use these commands for editing several files at the same time and for viewing several files on-screen. Each file is edited in an `emacs` *buffer* and can be visible in a *window*.

| Command | What It Does |
|---|---|
| Ctrl+x b | Switches to a different buffer for editing. |
| Ctrl+x Ctrl+f | Finds a file and reads it into a buffer for editing. |
| Ctrl+x k | Closes this buffer. If you haven't saved the file, `emacs` asks whether you want to save the file. |
| Ctrl+x i | Inserts a file into the current file at the cursor position. |
| Ctrl+x o | Switches to the other window. |
| Ctrl+x Ctrl+s | Saves the current buffer into its file. |
| Ctrl+x 1 | Unsplits the screen so that only one window is visible. This command doesn't close any buffers. |
| Ctrl+x 2 | Splits the screen into two windows so that you can view two files at once. |

# Using the pico Text Editor

`pico` is a simple, easy-to-use text editor. Commands are listed at the bottom of the screen as a reference.

TIP

`pico` is relatively new and may not be available on some systems. If it is, use it — because it's easy!

## Starting pico

To start `pico`, simply type **pico** at the shell prompt.

To create a new file and give it a name or to load an existing file, type

```
pico filename
```

`pico` displays the first screen of the file. The cursor is at the beginning of the file.

## Getting out of pico

1. Press Ctrl+x.
2. `pico` prompts you to save your work. Press Y to save or N to exit without saving.

## pico commands

You type commands by holding down the Control (Ctrl) key and pressing a letter.

The following commands are available in `pico`. The corresponding function key commands are shown in parentheses.

| Command | What It Does |
|---|---|
| Ctrl+g (F1) | Displays the help screen. |
| Ctrl+f | Moves the cursor forward one character. |
| Ctrl+b | Moves the cursor backward one character. |
| Ctrl+p | Moves the cursor to the preceding line. |
| Ctrl+n | Moves the cursor to the next line. |
| Ctrl+a | Moves the cursor to the beginning of the current line. |
| Ctrl+e | Moves the cursor to the end of the current line. |
| Ctrl+v (F8) | Moves the cursor forward a page of text. |
| Ctrl+y (F7) | Moves the cursor backward one page of text. |
| Ctrl+w (F6) | Searches for text within the file. |
| Ctrl+l | Refreshes the display. |
| Ctrl+d | Deletes the character under the cursor. |
| Ctrl+k (F9) | Cuts the line of text at the cursor position. |
| Ctrl+u (F10) | Uncuts (pastes) text, inserting it at the cursor position. |

*(continued)*

| Command | What It Does |
|---|---|
| Ctrl+i | Inserts a tab at the cursor position. |
| Ctrl+j (F4) | Reformats the current paragraph as justified text. |
| Ctrl+t (F12) | Runs the spelling checker. |
| Ctrl+c (F11) | Displays the number of lines of text that exist. |
| Ctrl+r (F5) | Inserts ("reads") an existing file at the cursor position. |
| Ctrl+o (F3) | Saves ("outputs") the text to a file. |
| Ctrl+x (F2) | Exits `pico`, prompting you to save the file. |

TIP

The online `pico` help screens display the ^ character to represent the Ctrl key. The online help also displays capital letters in commands. Therefore, if the help screen tells you to type **^B**, you should hold down the Ctrl key and press b.

# Using the vi Text Editor

`vi` is a widely used, powerful screen editor based on `ed` that is available on almost all systems. You use it to edit text files, including writing e-mail messages or shell scripts.

## Starting vi

To start `vi`, simply type **vi** at the shell prompt.

To create a new file and give it a name or to load an existing file, type

```
vi filename
```

`vi` displays the first screen of the file. If the file isn't long enough to fill the screen, `vi` shows tildes (~) on the blank lines. The cursor is at the beginning of the file.

`vi` is always in either *command mode* or *input mode* (also called *insert mode*). In command mode, the letters you type are interpreted as commands. In input mode, what you type is entered in the file you're editing.

To switch from command mode to input mode, use an `a` or `i` command (described later in this part) to tell `vi` where to put the new text.

To switch from input mode to command mode, press the Esc key. Press it a few times just to be sure. (`vi` just beeps when you press Esc when you're already in command mode.)

TIP

To run a marginally friendlier version of `vi`, try typing **vedit**. The `vedit` program displays various helpful messages, including messages that tell you when you are in input or command mode.

## Getting out of vi

1. If you're in input mode, press the Esc key to get into command mode.
2. Type **ZZ** to quit the program (those are *capital* Zs).

If you want to exit `vi` without saving the changes you made to the file, type **:q!** to quit without saving.

## vi commands

TIP

Most `vi` commands consist of one letter. Be sure to use either capital or lowercase letters as shown — in many cases, a capital letter does something rather different from the same lowercase letter!

| Command | What It Does |
|---|---|
| Esc | Returns to command mode from input mode. In command mode, `vi` just beeps. |
| Enter | Moves the cursor to the beginning of the next line. |
| 0 (zero) | Moves the cursor to the beginning of the current line. |
| $ | Moves the cursor to the end of the current line. |
| + | Moves the cursor to the beginning of the next line. |
| - | Moves the cursor to the beginning of the preceding line. |
| ) | Moves the cursor to the beginning of the next sentence. (A sentence ends with a period, exclamation point, or question mark followed by two spaces.) |
| ( | Moves the cursor to the beginning of the current sentence. |
| } | Moves the cursor to the beginning of the next paragraph. (A paragraph ends with a blank line.) |
| { | Moves the cursor to the beginning of the current paragraph. |
| /*text* | Searches forward through the file for the *text*. |
| / | Repeats the same search, searching forward. |
| ? | Repeats the same search, searching backward. |
| :!*command* | Runs a shell command and then returns to `vi`. |
| a | Adds text (that is, switches to input mode so that the text you type is added immediately after the cursor). |

*(continued)*

| *Command* | *What It Does* |
|---|---|
| A | Adds text at the end of the current line, switching to input mode. |
| b or B | Moves the cursor backward one word. |
| dd | Deletes the entire current line. |
| *n*dd | Deletes the next *n* lines. |
| D | Deletes the text from the cursor to the end of the line. |
| d ^ | Deletes the text from the cursor to the beginning of the line. |
| dw | Deletes the next word. |
| d) | Deletes to the end of the sentence. |
| d} | Deletes to the end of the paragraph. |
| dG | Deletes to the end of the file. (Watch out!) |
| e or E | Moves the cursor to the end of the word. |
| G | Goes (moves the cursor) to the end of the file. |
| 1G | Moves the cursor to the beginning of the file. |
| *nn*G | Moves the cursor to line *nn* of the file. |
| h | Moves the cursor left one character. |
| H | Moves the cursor to the top line of the screen. |
| i | Inserts text (that is, switches to input mode so that the text you type is inserted immediately before the cursor). |
| I | Inserts text at the beginning of the current line, switching to input mode. |
| j | Moves the cursor down one line. |
| k | Moves the cursor up one line. |
| l | Moves the cursor right one character. |
| L | Moves the cursor to the bottom line of the screen. |
| n | Repeats the last search (made with /). |
| N | Repeats the last search (made with /), searching in the opposite direction. |
| o | Opens (creates) a new line after the current line, switching to input mode so that you can type text on it. |
| O (the letter) | Opens a new line before the current line, switching to input mode so that you can type text on it. |
| p | Inserts ("puts") text deleted by the last y or Y command. The text is added just after the cursor. |
| P | Inserts text deleted by the last y or Y command just before the cursor. |
| :q! (followed by Enter) | Exits from the program without saving your changes. |

:set nu
:<#1>,<#2>d (delete code/y #1 a #2)



| *Command* | *What It Does* |
|---|---|
| R | Replaces text, switching to input mode so that the text you type replaces the text that is currently to the right of the cursor (also called *overtype* mode). |
| :sh | Runs the shell while putting vi on hold. To return from the shell, type **exit** or press Ctrl+D. You return to `vi` with the same file loaded and your cursor in the same position. Be sure to save your file before trying this command. |
| u | Undoes the last change. |
| U | Undoes all changes made to the current line since you moved to it. |
| w or W | Moves the cursor forward one word. |
| :w (followed by Enter) | Writes (saves) the file. |
| :wq (followed by Enter) | Exits from `vi` and saves any changes to the file (same as ZZ). |
| x | Deletes the character under the cursor. |
| X | Deletes the character to the left of the cursor. |
| :x (followed by Enter) | Exits `vi` and saves any changes to the file. |
| *n*x | Deletes the next *n* characters. |
| *n*X | Deletes the preceding *n* characters. |
| yy or Y | Copies ("yanks") the current line to a buffer for later use and deletes the line from the file. |
| yw | Copies the current word to a buffer for later use and deletes the word from the file. |
| y) | Copies the current sentence to a buffer for later use and deletes the sentence from the file. |
| y} | Copies the current paragraph to a buffer for later use and deletes the paragraph from the file. |
| ZZ | Exits from `vi` and saves any changes to the file (same as :wq). |
| Ctrl+Z | Suspends `vi` and returns to the UNIX shell. Resume `vi` by typing **fg**. |
| Ctrl+B | Scrolls backward one screen. |
| Ctrl+F | Scrolls forward one screen. |
| *:ed-command* | You can do any `ed` command in `vi` by typing a colon and the `ed` command and then pressing Enter. |

There are lots of other `vi` commands — almost every letter is a command. Be careful what you type while you're in command mode! And be sure to use capital and small letters in commands just as they're listed in the table.

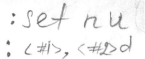

## vi commands in input mode

| *Command* | *What It Does* |
|---|---|
| Esc | Returns to command mode from input mode (Ctrl+C does this, too). |
| Ctrl+U | Scrolls backward one screen. |
| Ctrl+D | Scrolls forward one screen. |
| Ctrl+H | Backspaces. |
| Ctrl+J | Moves the cursor down one line. |
| Ctrl+W | Moves the cursor backward to the beginning of the word. |

Part V

# Sending and Receiving Electronic Mail

Every UNIX system comes with some sort of mail system. At worst, you have a primitive mail program and can send mail only to other users on your machine. At best, you use a much better mail program (probably elm or Pine) and can send mail to anyone on the Internet.

## *In this part . . .*

- **Using elm, a popular screen-based mail program**
- **Using Mail, the basic mail program that comes with most UNIX systems**
- **Using Pine, an easy-to-use, full-featured mail program**

For each program, we show you how to send, read, and save mail.

# Addressing Your Mail

When you address your mail, you enter the *mail address* of the person to whom you want to send mail.

Every user has a mail address, usually the same as the user (login) name. If your computer is attached to a network, your mail address is your username, an at sign (@), and the name of your computer — `betsy@marketing`, for example. System administrators can set up other mail addresses for mailing lists, remote users, and other purposes.

Some systems that run the ancient uucp network software use an exclamation point in place of the @, as in `marketing!betsy`.

# elm

To run the program, type **elm** at the shell prompt. You see the *message index,* a nice listing of your messages with one message per line. At the bottom of the screen is a list of the elm commands you can use.

***See also*** *UNIX For Dummies,* 4th Edition, Chapter 17, and *MORE UNIX For Dummies,* Chapter 18.

## Sending a message

1. Type **elm**.
2. Press m.
3. elm asks whom to send the message to. Type a mail address.
4. elm prompts you for the message subject. Enter one.
5. elm may ask for addresses to which you want to send copies of the message. Type the names if you want to include any. (Type your own username if you want to keep a copy for yourself.) Just press Enter or Return if you don't want to send any copies.
6. elm runs a text editor, usually `vi`. Type your message.
7. After completing your message, give the commands to save the completed message and exit the editor. In `vi`, type **ZZ** or **:x**. In `emacs`, press Ctrl+X, Ctrl+S, Ctrl+X, Ctrl+C.

   elm asks something like this:

   ```
   Please choose one of the following options by
     parenthesized letter:
   e)dit message, !)shell, h)eaders, c)opy file,
     s)end,or f)orget.
   ```

You have the choice of pressing s to send the message, h to edit the header lines, e to go back and edit the message some more, c to copy a file into the message, ! to run a shell command, or f to forget it and throw away the message.

8. To send the message, press s. elm sends the message and displays the list of messages in your mailbox again.

TIP: If you would rather use `emacs` or `pico` than `vi` as your text editor, ask your system administrator to set up elm to run that editor or see the section "Changing your elm options" later in this part.

## Reading your messages

1. Type **elm** at the shell prompt. You see the message index.

2. Press the cursor keys to move the cursor to the message you want. If the message is off the bottom of the screen (because you have more messages than can fit, you popular person), press the spacebar to see each subsequent screen of messages or use the cursor keys to scroll through the list. If your cursor keys don't work, press j to move forward and k to move backward.

3. Press Enter to view the message. If the message is too long to fit on-screen, press the spacebar to see more of it.

4. After you finish reading the message, decide whether you want to keep it. Press d to delete the message and go on to the next one. To keep it, press the up- or down-arrow key (or j and k) to go to preceding or subsequent messages without deleting anything.

5. To stop reading messages, press i to return to the message index.

## Printing a message

This task prints a message on a printer connected to the UNIX system. If you dial in from a PC, this process won't do what you want — instead, you have to save the message to a file, download the file, and then print the downloaded file.

1. Type **elm**. You see the message index.

2. Press the cursor keys (or j and k) to select the message you want to print.

3. Press p. The message is printed.

## Saving a message

You can use elm to store messages in a text file for later perusing, editing, printing, or other uses.

1. Type **elm**. You see the message index.
2. Press the cursor keys (or j and k) to select the message you want to save.
3. Press s.
4. Type the name of the file in which to save the message or press Enter to accept elm's suggested filename (usually the name of the sender).

TIP: Your mailbox usually resides in a subdirectory of your home directory called `Mail`. If you precede a filename with an equal sign, such as `=loveletters`, elm puts the file in your Mail directory. You can save multiple messages into one file; elm just adds the new messages to the end of the file.

## Exiting the program

To quit elm and save any changes you made to your mailbox, such as deleting messages:

1. Press q.
2. elm asks whether you want to save the messages you've already read. Press y or Enter to save them in a file named received, or press n to leave them in your mailbox. Either way, your messages are saved in one place or the other.

To quit elm without saving changes to your mailbox:

1. Press x.
2. If you made changes, elm asks whether you really want to exit without saving them.
3. Press y to exit without saving or n if you change your mind.

## Changing your elm options

You can customize elm so that it uses the editor you like, displays messages in the order you want, and does other things. To customize, follow these steps:

1. Type **elm**. You see the message index.
2. To see your elm options, press o. elm displays a list of its options, along with your setting for each one. You should leave most of these settings alone so that you don't break elm.

3. To use a different editor for composing messages, press e. Your cursor jumps to the name of the editor that elm currently runs when you want to send a message. Edit this program name and press Enter. Notice that it is a full pathname; ask your system administrator to tell you the full pathname of the editor you want to use. Then press Enter.

4. To change the order in which messages are displayed in the message index, press s. Then press the spacebar repeatedly until you see the ordering you want. Press r to switch between forward and reverse orders. (Our favorite is Date Mail Sent, sorting from least recent to most recent.) Then press Enter.

5. To change other settings, press the letter that appears in front of the parenthesis at the beginning of its line. Make the change and then press Enter.

6. When you finish messing around with the options, type > to save your changes. If you think that you may have made a mistake, skip this step.

7. To return to your elm message index, press i.

## Getting help

To see online help in elm, type **?**. Typing another question mark displays a list of all the commands.

## Command line options

`elm [-f file] [-h] [-s subject] -v [recipients]`

| *Option or Argument* | *Function* |
|---|---|
| -f *file* | Reads mail from *file* rather than from your usual mailbox. |
| -h | Displays help about the elm program. |
| -s *subject* | Sets the subject when sending mail (applies only if you also specify a recipient for sending mail without first seeing the message index). |
| -v | Reports elm's version number. |
| *recipients* | Sets the name(s) of the recipient(s) when you're sending mail. This option is for sending mail without first seeing the message index. |

# Mail

Mail is the basic mail program that comes with all UNIX systems. It may be named mail, or it may be called mailx or Mail. You use the same program with different arguments to send and receive mail.

If your system has mailx or Mail, there may be another, even older mail program that you don't want to use.

In our examples, we use the Mail (uppercase M) program; substitute **mail** (lowercase m) or **mailx** if you use either of those programs.

## Sending a message

1. Run your mail program and give it the name(s) of the mail recipients, like this:

   ```
   Mail elvis@ntw.org
   ```

2. Depending on how the mail program is configured, it may prompt you for a subject line. If so, type one:

   ```
   Subject: Hound dogs
   ```

   If it doesn't ask for a subject and you want to provide one, type **~s** followed by the subject:

   ```
   ~sHound dogs
   ```

3. Type your message.
4. When you're finished entering the text of the message, type a period on a line by itself. The mail program responds with EOT. (Some ancient versions don't understand the period; for them, press Ctrl+D.) UNIX sends the message.

While you're sending mail, the editing commands in the following table are available. You start each command with a tilde (~) on a new, blank line.

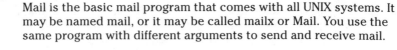

| *Command* | *What It Does* |
|---|---|
| ~b *name* | Adds a name to the blind carbon copy list. |
| ~c *name* | Adds a name to the carbon copy list. |
| ~e | Runs a text editor (usually `vi`) to edit the message. |
| ~f | Forwards the current message from the mailbox to someone else. |
| ~p | Prints (displays on-screen) the message so far. |
| ~q | Quits and abandons this message. |

| Command | What It Does |
| --- | --- |
| ~r *file* | Reads in the contents of *file*. |
| ~s *subject* | Sets the message subject. |
| ~c *name* | Adds *name* to the list of recipients. |
| ~v | Visual edit: Runs the `vi` editor so that you can edit the message. |
| ~w *file* | Writes the current message to a file. |
| ~. | Ends the message and delivers it. |

TIP

If you want to save a copy of a message you're sending, include your own username in the blind carbon copy list by using the `~b` command.

## Reading your messages

1. Run your mail program by typing **Mail**, **mail**, or **mailx**. The mail program shows you your new messages followed by a question-mark prompt, like this:

```
mailx version 3.1  Type ? for help.
"/usr/mail/johnl": 21 messages 1 new
>N 21 elvis Thu Dec 16 15:59   17/361
Club date
?
```

2. To read each new message, press Enter. If a message is more than one page long, press the spacebar or Return to move through the message.
3. After reading a message, decide whether you want to save it. At the ? prompt, press d to delete it or type **dp** to delete it and display the next message. To keep the message and display the next, press Enter.

## Forwarding a message

To send a copy of an incoming message to a third party:

1. After you read a message, press m to tell the program that you want to create a new message.
2. Immediately after the `m`, type the address to which you want to forward the message.
3. Enter an appropriate subject when asked.
4. Type **~m** on a separate line to insert the original message into the mail you're sending.
5. Enter more text if you want to and then type a period on a separate line or press Ctrl+D to finish.

## Printing a message

The Mail program doesn't have a built-in printing command, but you can tell it to send the message to the standard printing program. Within the Mail program on BSD UNIX systems, type this line:

```
| lpr
```

(That's a vertical bar, a space, and the `lpr` command.)

On UNIX System V, type this line:

```
| lp
```

## Saving a message

With Mail, you can store messages in a text file for later perusing, editing, printing, or other uses. To save a message, follow these steps:

1. Run your mail program. It shows you your new messages.
2. Select the message you want either by pressing Enter until the message you want appears or by typing the message number and then pressing Enter.
3. Type **s**, a space, and the name of the file in which to save the message.

TIP: You can save as many messages as you want in a single file. That file can be treated as a mailbox; use `Mail -f` *`filename`* to tell Mail to read its contents.

## Exiting the mail program

Press q to quit and save changes to your mailbox.

Press x to exit and discard changes to your mailbox.

## Command line options

`Mail [-f` *`file`*`] [-N] [-H] [-s` *`subject`*`] [`*`recipients`*`]`

| Option or Argument | Function |
|---|---|
| -f *file* | Reads your mail from the mailbox file you specify. |
| -N | Doesn't list message headers when it starts. |
| -H | Lists only the messages headers and then exits. |
| -s *subject* | Sets the subject when sending mail. |
| *recipients* | Sets the name(s) of the recipient(s) when you're sending mail. |

# Pine

Pine is an easy-to-use menu-driven mail program. It uses folders to store incoming mail and addresses. It also lets you send *attachments,* which are nontext files such as graphics files or spreadsheets.

To start Pine, type **pine** at the shell prompt. You see the *Main menu.* At the bottom of the screen is a list of Pine commands you can use.

| Command | What It Does |
|---|---|
| ? | Shows the help screen. |
| c | Composes and sends a message. |
| i | Displays messages in the current folder. |
| l | Selects a folder to view. |
| a | Creates or modifies address books. |
| s | Accesses setup options. |
| q | Quits Pine. |
| o | Shows all other available commands. |
| p | Selects the preceding item displayed on the menu. |
| n | Selects the next item displayed on the menu. |
| r | Displays release notes, which contain information for using Pine. |
| k | Locks the keyboard, preventing others from accessing it when you are not at your computer. |
| g | Goes to a specified folder. |

***See also*** Chapter 17 of *UNIX For Dummies,* 4th Edition, and Chapter 18 of *MORE UNIX For Dummies.*

## Sending a message

1. Type **pine** at the shell prompt.
2. Press c (for *compose*) to display the Compose Message screen.
3. In the Address field, type a mail address and press Enter. You can type several names if desired, with a comma separating them.
4. In the Cc: field, enter the addresses of other people you want to receive the message. Press Enter.

5. The Attachment field lets you send a file that is not a text file (such as a graphics file or word processing document). Enter the pathname of the file here (if the file is in your home directory, you can just type the filename) or press Ctrl+T to select from a menu of your files. Then press Enter.

6. In the Subject field, briefly describe the message and press Enter.

7. Type your message. Pine uses the `pico` editor described in Part IV. If you want to send a file that you previously wrote, press Ctrl+R to read in a file. Enter the pathname of the file here (if the file is in your home directory, you can just type the filename) or press Ctrl+T to select from a menu of your files.

8. To send your message, press Ctrl+X.

   Pine asks:

   ```
   Send message?
   ```

9. Press y (for *yes*) or Enter. The message is sent, and a copy of it is saved in the sent mail folder.

## Reading your messages

New messages are stored in the INBOX folder. To read them:

1. Type **pine** at the shell prompt. The Main menu appears.

2. At the Main menu, press i (for *index*). A list of mail messages appears.

3. Use the arrow keys to highlight the message you want to view or press p or n to move up or down a message. Press v (for *view*) or Enter to read a selected message.

4. To return to the index, press i again.

The left side of the INBOX screen shows the status of the messages as follows:

| | |
|---|---|
| n | The message is new. |
| + | The message was sent directly to you (as opposed to coming via a mailing list or a Cc: of a message to someone else). |
| d | You have read the message and marked it for deletion. |
| a | You responded to this message by using the Reply feature. |

## Replying to a message

To reply to a message you are reading, follow these steps:

1. Press r (for *reply*).

   You are asked whether you want to include the original message in your reply. Also, if the original message was sent to more than one person, you are asked whether you want to reply to all recipients.

2. Enter the text of your message.

3. To send your message, press Ctrl+X.

   Pine asks:

   ```
   Send message?
   ```

4. Press y (for *yes*) or Enter.

## Forwarding a message

To forward a message that you have selected at the Index screen or that you are viewing, follow these steps:

1. Press f (for *forward*). A copy of the message opens and the To: field is highlighted.

2. Enter the address of your recipient and send the message as usual. Note that you can modify the original message if you wish.

## Printing a message

To print messages from either the Folder Index screen or the View Message screen, press y.

The first time you print, you may have to adjust your Pine configuration to get printing to work. Pine provides three options for printing. Do not change these settings if you can print successfully.

To choose the printing method that Pine uses, follow these steps:

1. At the Pine Main menu, press s (for *setup*).

2. Press p (for *printer*).

   Pine displays three options:

   - PC and Macintosh printing
   - UNIX printing
   - A custom print command

3. Enter **1**, **2**, or **3** to select one of the three printing methods. You may be required to enter a command that will be used to access the printer.

## Saving a message

Pine provides three storage places for messages:

- The INBOX folder stores new messages sent to you.
- The saved messages folder stores copies of saved messages.
- The sent mail folder automatically copies and stores messages you send.

You can also create your own folders based on subject matter or name of correspondent. To create a new folder, follow these steps:

1. At the Main menu, press i (for *index*).
2. At the INBOX screen, press l (for *list* folders).
3. At the Folders List, press a (for *add*).
4. Enter the name of the new folder and press Enter.

When you save a message, you can store it in the saved messages folder, or you can specify another folder:

1. On the Index menu, use the arrow keys or press p or n to highlight the message you want to save.
2. Press s (for *save*) to save the message. You can also press e (for *export*) to save the message to a file in your home directory.
3. If you press s, you're asked whether you want to save the message to the saved messages folder, which is the default. If you want to save the message to the default folder, press Enter. If you'd rather save the message to another folder, enter the name of the folder and then press Enter.

Once you save a message, the message in the INBOX folder is automatically marked for deletion. When you quit Pine, you're asked whether you want to permanently delete the message from the INBOX folder.

## Deleting a message

Pine lets you delete and undelete messages. To mark for deletion a message that you don't want, follow these steps:

1. On the Folder Index screen, use the arrow keys or press p or n to highlight the message you want to delete.

2. Press d (for *delete*).
3. If you change your mind about a message that you have marked for deletion, press u (for *undelete*) to restore the message.

A message that is marked for deletion will not be deleted until you "expunge" it, or permanently delete it. To expunge deleted messages, follow these steps:

1. On the Folder Index screen, press x (for *expunge*).

   Pine asks:

   `Expunge message(s)"?`

2. Press y or the Enter key.

## Adding an address to an address book

Pine lets you store the addresses of individuals or groups that you can then easily retrieve when you write new messages:

1. At the Pine Main menu, press a (for *address* book).
2. To add a single address, press a (for *add*).
3. Enter the name, nickname, and e-mail address(es) when Pine prompts you to do so.

By entering a short nickname, you can just type the nickname when you write a message. Pine automatically retrieves the full address.

## Retrieving an address from an address book

When addressing mail, you can retrieve e-mail addresses stored in an address book. In the To: or Cc: of the message header, follow these steps:

1. Press Ctrl+T.
2. Press the P or N keys or arrow keys to highlight the address you want to use.
3. Press s (for *select*) or Enter.

## Exiting the program

To quit Pine, follow these steps:

1. At almost any place in Pine, press q (for *quit*).

   Pine asks:

   `Really quit pine?`

2. Press y or Enter to quit.

### Changing options

You can customize Pine options, such as printer, name and location of folders, and other things. In general, don't change these options unless you need to. Here's how to customize:

1. Type **pine**. The Main menu appears.
2. Press s (for *setup*). Pine displays four options:
   - **Printer:** Chooses a printer.
   - **Newpassword:** Changes your account password.
   - **Config:** Modifies such things as pathnames to mail folders and address books. You can also change your name as it appears in messages.
   - **Update:** Provide information about updates to Pine.
3. Press p, n, c, or u to select the desired screen.
4. Use the arrows keys or press p or n to highlight the option you want to change.
5. To modify a setting, press c (for *change*), a (for *add*, and enter a new value), or x (for *set/unset*).
6. To return to the Pine Main menu, press e.

### Getting help

To view the help screen, use the Help command at the bottom of each screen. It's usually ? or Ctrl+G, depending on the screen.

## Sending Mail Using Other Mail Programs

If you are using X Windows and want a mail program with lots of buttons and icons, many other programs allow you to perform most mailing operations with mouse clicks. Check with your system administrator to see which of these, if any, are installed on your system. (Netscape, which is a ubiquitous browser on UNIX systems, comes with an X-based mailer, too. Its mail program on UNIX works just like it does on Windows or a Mac. See *Internet For Dummies Quick Reference,* 4th Edition.

Details vary, but the steps are generally similar to those outlined for the three programs described in this part.

1. Tell the program that you want to send a message.
2. Give the address to send the message to.
3. Enter the message and subject.
4. Tell the program that you're done composing the message.

Part VI

# Connecting to Other Computers

Several facilities can put you into direct contact with other computers on the Internet. This part describes some of the methods you can use.

## In this part . . .

- **Using FTP and `rcp` to copy files to and retrieve files from other computers**
- **Using anonymous FTP to connect to Internet systems**
- **Using IRC to chat with other users on the Net**
- **Using `rlogin` and `rsh` to log in to other computers on the Net as though you were connected to them directly**
- **Using `telnet` to connect to and disconnect from remote computers**

# FTP

FTP, or File Transfer Protocol, lets you copy files between your computer and other computers on the network.

## Connecting to a remote system

Use the following procedure to log in to a computer on the Net for the purpose of copying files to or from your computer:

1. Run the FTP program, giving it the name of the system to connect to by typing **ftp** followed by the name of the system to connect to.
2. A message confirming that you are connected appears. Then the program asks for a login name and password. If you have an account on that system, use the same name and password you use for a direct or `telnet` login. The screen looks like the following:

   ```
   Connected to shamu.ntw.org.
   220 FTP server (Version 4.1 8/1/91) ready.
   Name: type your login name here
   331 Password required for elvis.
   Password: type password here
   ```

On most systems, you can create a file called `.netrc` (or plain `Netrc` on non-UNIX systems). This file contains the login name for each system that you use often. Each line lists a machine, the login name, and the password for that machine, like this:

```
machine shamu.ntw.org login king password sinatra
```

When you FTP to that system, it logs you in automatically.

Notice that using a `.netrc` file requires you to type your password in the file; generally this is something that you should avoid if at all possible for security reasons, so many system administrators frown on this procedure. If you do use a `.netrc` file, be sure the protections on the file are set to 0600 so nobody else can see your passwords.

On some versions of FTP, you can place a default line at the end of the `.netrc` file to say what login name to use for systems that are not listed:

```
default login anonymous password elvis@ntw.org
```

## Connecting by using anonymous FTP

Anonymous FTP lets you connect to Internet systems that make files available to the public. On those systems, rather than logging in with your own name, you log in as **anonymous** and use your e-mail address, or the word *guest,* as the password:

1. Run the FTP program.
2. When the remote computer asks for your login name, type **anonymous**.
3. When the remote computer prompts you for your password, enter your e-mail address. If the system suggests *guest* as the password, type **guest** instead. The prompts appear as follows:

```
ftp internic.net
Connected to internic.net.
220 *****Welcome to the InterNIC Registration Host
   *****
Name: anonymous
331 Guest login ok, send "guest" as password.
Password: type e-mail address or guest here
230 Guest login ok, access restrictions apply.
```

## Quitting FTP

To disconnect from the remote computer, type **quit**.

## Listing the files in a directory

After you log in by using FTP, you need to look for the files you want to retrieve.

1. Type **dir**, which is short for *directory.*
2. You see lots of messages, including a list of the files and subdirectories in the current directory. Following is a listing of the messages that appear:

```
ftp> dir
200 PORT command successful.
150 Opening ASCII mode data connection for /
  bin/ls.
total 23
drwxrwxr-x 19 root  archive     512 Jun 24
  12:09 doc
drwxrwxr-x  5 root  archive     512 May 18
  08:14 edu
drwxr-xr-x 31 root  wheel  512 Jul 12 10:37
  systems
drwxr-xr-x  3 root  archive     512 Jun 25
  1992 vendorware
...lots of other stuff...
226 Transfer complete.
1341 bytes received in 0.77 seconds (1.7
  Kbytes/s)
```

If the directory is so big that it doesn't fit on-screen, you can ask for just part of the directory by using wildcards. For example, `dir c*` asks for just the files whose names start with the letter *c*.

TIP

If you want to store the directory listing on your own computer, you can enter the name of a local file in which to store the listing. Use the `dir` command, followed by a period (to indicate that you want a listing of the current directory), followed by the filename in which to store the result, like this:

```
ftp> dir . file-list
200 PORT command successful.
150 Opening ASCII mode data connection for /bin/ls.
226 Transfer complete.
45341 bytes received in 42 seconds (1.0 Kbytes/s)
```

## Moving to other directories

Use the following procedure to change directories on the remote computer:

1. Type **cd** and the name of the directory to change to. For example:

   ```
   ftp> cd edu
   250 CWD command successful.
   ```

2. Use the `dir` command to see what's in the new directory.

On many systems, the interesting stuff is stored in a directory called `pub`.

## Retrieving files

To copy files from the remote computer to your own computer, you first need to set yourself up to retrieve the files. Then you retrieve them by using the `get` command.

1. Use the `cd` command to move to the directory where the file(s) you want are located on the remote computer.

2. If the files are not plain text, type **bin** to tell FTP to transfer the files as binary files, not text files.

   ```
   ftp> bin
   200 Type set to I.
   ```

3. Type **get**, the filename on the remote computer, and the filename to use on your computer (the local filename). If you want to use the same name, you can omit the local filename. Following is what appears on-screen (in this example, you want to get the file `intro.txt` and rename it as `intro-file` on your machine):

```
ftp> get intro.txt intro-file
local: intro-file remote: intro.txt
200 PORT command successful.
150 Opening ASCII mode data connection for
  intro.txt (5243 bytes).
226 Transfer complete.
5359 bytes received in 0 seconds (5.2 Kbytes/s)
```

FTP retrieves the file and displays a message about it.

FTP can take a long time to retrieve a large file. For a file retrieved from a distant site over a dial-up connection, allow one second for every 1,000 characters in the file.

If you retrieve a nontext file and it arrives smashed and unusable, 95 percent of the time you forgot to type **bin** before you retrieved it.

## *Retrieving groups of files*

To copy a group of files with one `mget` command, do the following:

1. Move to the directory that contains the files and, if appropriate, set binary mode, as we describe in the preceding section.
2. Type **mget** (for multiple get), followed by the names of the files to get. You can also use patterns — notably *, which means all files in the directory.
3. `mget` asks you about each file that matches the names and patterns in the list. Press y to transfer the file or n to skip it.

Use the `prompt` command before any `mget` commands to turn off the prompting for each file so that all the files in the group transfer without asking first.

## *Decompressing files that you have retrieved*

Files on anonymous FTP systems are usually stored in one of several forms that save space and make them easier to transfer, but you need to decode them in order to use them.

The *filename extension* (the part after the dot) tells you how the file is coded and, more important, which program you need to use to decode the file. See Part II for how to use these decoding programs.

Following is a table of common file types:

| *Type* | *Description* |
|---|---|
| Text | Plain text that can be printed, displayed, and edited with the usual printing and text editing programs. |
| Compressed | A coded form, with many variants, that saves space. |
| Archived | Many files combined into one. (Most archived files are also compressed.) |
| Images | Digitized pictures in GIF, JPEG, or other image format. |

Most file types are identified by an extension.

| *Extension* | *Description* |
|---|---|
| uu | Special uuencoded format that disguises a nontext file as text so it can be e-mailed. |
| Z | Z files (capital Z) are compressed files created by the UNIX compress program and are decoded with `uncompress`. |
| gz | gz and z files are created by the GNU `gzip` program and uncompressed by GNU `gunzip`. GNU `gunzip` knows about a great deal of compression formats and can decode most compressed formats that aren't also archive formats. |
| tar | `tar` (Tape ARchive) is a UNIX archiving program. To unpack a tar file on a UNIX system, type **tar xvf blurfle.tar**. tar files are commonly compressed with names like blurfle.tar.Z. Uncompress them and then `untar` them. On some systems, tar files are called .taz files. |
| cpio | `cpio` (CoPy In and Out) is another UNIX program with its own format. To decode it on a UNIX system, type **cpio -itcv < blurfle.cpio**. Compressed `cpio` is also common. Uncompress the file and then `uncpio` it. |
| zip | zip files are the most common kind of compressed archives used on DOS and Windows systems. You extract files from them by using the widely available `unzip` command: **unzip blurfle.zip**. |

## Downloading retrieved files to your PC

If you are using a local PC to dial into an Internet host, FTP retrieves files to the Internet host, not to your local PC. After the files are on your Internet host, you have to download them to your PC.

Downloading details vary, but (generally speaking) you do the following:

1. Type the command to the host to start the downloading program, such as **sz** for Zmodem or **kermit** for Kermit, and type the names of the files to download.

2. If your PC terminal program doesn't start downloading automatically, you need to tell it to start downloading, typically by using an Alt+key combination. If you don't know the appropriate key combination, refer to your terminal program's manual.

3. After the files are downloaded, delete the copies on the Internet host so that you aren't charged for the disk space.

The HyperTerminal program that comes with Microsoft Windows 95 and 98 can transfer binary files by using Xmodem, Ymodem, Zmodem, or Kermit. To send a file, use `Transfer Send file` and choose the file to send and the protocol to use from the pop-up menu. To receive a file, use `Transfer Receive file`.

HyperTerminal handles Zmodem automatically. Just type the **sz** ***filename*** command to UNIX and Hyperterminal downloads the file without further commands.

## *Sending files to a remote system using FTP*

If the permissions allow, you can send files to a remote system. A common reason to upload files to a UNIX system is to put Web pages onto a Web server.

1. Use the **cd** command to move to the directory in which you want to store the file on the remote computer.

2. If the files contain binary data, set binary mode, as we describe in the earlier "Retrieving files" section.

3. Type **put**, the filename on your computer (the local filename), and the filename to use on the remote system. You can omit the remote filename if it's the same as the local filename. The following appears on-screen. (In this example, you are uploading a file called `nigel` and renaming it as `nigel-data` on the way.)

```
ftp> put nigel nigel-data
local: myfile remote: stored-file
200 PORT command successful.
150 Opening ASCII mode data connection for
  nigel-data.
226 Transfer complete.
795 bytes sent in 0 seconds (0.78 Kbytes/s)
```

You can copy a group of files to the remote computer by using the `mput` command. In Step 3, type **mput** and the name of the files to store or a pattern that matches the name of the files to store. The pattern * means all files in the local directory.

As it copies the files, `mput` asks you about each file. Press y to store a file or n to skip it.

TIP: If you want to store a group of files without FTP asking you about each one, type **prompt** before any **mput** commands to turn off name prompting.

## Summary of FTP commands

Here's a short list of useful FTP commands, including a few not otherwise mentioned:

| *Command* | *Description* |
|---|---|
| `get` *old new* | Copy remote file *old* to local file *new*. You can omit *new* if it has the same name as *old*. |
| `put` *old new* | Copy local file *old* to remote file *new*. You can omit *new* if it has the same name as *old*. |
| `del` *xyz* | Delete file *xyz* on a remote system. |
| `cd` *newdir* | Change to directory *newdir* on the remote machine. |
| `cdup` | Change to the next higher directory (the parent directory). |
| `lcd` *newdir* | Change to the directory *newdir* on the local machine. |
| `asc` | Transfer files in ASCII mode. (Use for text files.) |
| `bin` | Transfer files in binary or image mode. (Use for all other files.) |
| `quit` | Leave FTP. |
| `dir` *pat* | List files whose names match the pattern *pat*. If you omit *pat*, list all files. |
| `mget` *pat* | Get files whose names match the pattern *pat*. |
| `mput` *pat* | Put files whose names match the pattern *pat*. |
| `mdel` *pat* | Delete remote files whose names match the pattern *pat*. |

# IRC: Chatting with Others on the Net

Internet Relay Chat (IRC) lets people across the Internet talk to one another live. Jarkko Oikarinen, at the University of Oulu Computing Center, Finland, originally wrote IRC.

IRC consists of many channels, or *chat areas,* where a group of people can discuss a particular subject. You can also have private conversations with one person. Each user has a nickname, which is either a made-up name or your login name.

There are three channel types, listed according to increasing levels of privacy:

- ✦ **Public:** Public channels are available to all users.
- ✦ **Secret:** Other users can tell that you are using IRC, but they can't see the name of the channel.
- ✦ **Hidden:** Other users can't see you or the channel.

## Starting IRC

To start IRC, type **irc** or **ircii** at the shell prompt, followed by the nickname you want to use on IRC and the name of your IRC server, for example:

```
irc BadBob irc.netcom.com
```

Two people cannot have the same nickname. If you select a nickname that's already in use, the system prompts you for a different nickname.

To start IRC and go to a particular channel, specify both a channel to enter and a nickname as follows: **irc "#cars" BadBob irc.netcom.com**. (You need to quote the # sign.)

If you don't specify a channel when you start IRC, information about the current IRC activity is displayed:

```
+/HELP NEWUSER
*** This server was created Nov 22 1992 at 19:02:56
    EST
*** There are 1003 users and 377 invisible on 146
    servers
*** 74 users have connection to the twilight zone
*** There are 374 channels.
*** I have 1 clients and 1 servers
```

You can now find out which channels are available and then join one.

## Finding IRC channels

To find out which IRC channels are available, type **/list**.

This command displays available channels, the number of users on each channel, and the subject matter of each channel. Secret and hidden channels do not appear.

Because there are many channels, the list that is shown may be quite long. You can shorten the list by typing the command **/list -MIN *numusers***. This list shows only channels with at least *numusers* users.

You can also use wildcards. To see all channels that start with the letter *d,* for example, type

```
/list #d*
```

## Joining an IRC channel

All channel names have a # before them.

To join a channel, type **/join #channel**. For example, to join the channel called `#fishing`, you type

```
/join #fishing
```

## Quitting IRC

Use any of the following commands to quit IRC: `/bye`, `/exit`, `/quit`, or `/signoff`.

## Getting help with IRC commands

If you need help with IRC commands, type **/help**. Help displays a list of available commands.

If you know the name of the command you want to use but can't remember what it does, type **/help *commandname***. Help displays information about the specified command.

To quit the Help mode, press Enter. Sometimes you have to press the Enter key several times.

TIP: Many advanced IRC commands exist but are not described in this section. You can create automated scripts to connect to IRC and even start up your own channel. If you want more information about IRC, a good place to look is the newsgroup `alt.irc`. ***See*** Part VIII for details about reading newsgroups.

## Chatting by using IRC commands

To *chat* with others, simply enter text and press Enter to send it to someone.

- ✦ A message that you send to everyone is displayed with a preceding `>`, and your nickname is displayed in angle brackets, as shown: `<BadBob> >Hello.`
- ✦ A message that you send privately to one person is displayed with a preceding `->`, and the nickname of the person you send it to appears in asterisks. For example, if you send the private message "Yikes!" to Eskimo Joe, it looks like this: `->*Eskimo Joe* Yikes!`

TIP

Other people on IRC may see different things on their screens because they may be using Windows or Mac-based programs like mIRC, Ircle, or Microsoft Chat, but the text that you and they type remains unchanged.

Here are a few editing commands you can use:

| *Command* | *Description* |
|---|---|
| Ctrl+A | Moves the cursor to the beginning of the line. |
| Ctrl+B | Moves the cursor back a character |
| Ctrl+D | Deletes the character under the cursor. |
| Ctrl+E | Goes to the end of the line. |
| Ctrl+F | Moves the cursor forward a character. |
| Ctrl+K | Deletes (kills) from the cursor to the end of the line. |

## Summary of IRC commands

Commands are preceded by /. Press Enter after you type the command.

| *Command* | *Description* |
|---|---|
| `/away` *`message`* | Tells other users that you will be away from your computer for a while. When you get back, type **/away** again to rejoin the conversation. |
| `/clear` | Clears the screen if it becomes cluttered. |
| `/invite` *`name channel`* | Lets you invite a user who is currently on IRC to join your channel. |
| `/join` *`channel`* | Joins the specified channel. The name of the channel must be a number. |
| `/list` | Displays a list of available channels, the topics of the channels, and the number of users on the channels. This command does not work for hidden or secret channels. |
| `/msg` *`name message`* | Sends a private message to the specified user. Other users cannot see this message. |
| `/nick` *`newnickname`* | Changes your nickname to the new one you enter. |
| `/query` *`name`* | Asks someone to have a private conversation. |

*(continued)*

| Command | Description |
|---|---|
| `/summon name` | Lets you summon a user who is not using IRC to enter the channel. You must enter the full login address of the user (such as `joe@computer.com`). |
| `/users` | Displays a list of the users logged in to the system. |
| `/who channel` | Lists all the users on the channel you specify. |
| `/whois name` | Displays the login name and host computer name of the specified user. |

### Having an IRC private conversation

If you have a private conversation with another user, only the two of you can see anything typed. The other person does not have to be on the same channel as you, but does have to be using IRC.

To ask another user to enter into a private conversation, type **/query *name***, where *name* is the nickname of the other user. If the other user repeats the command by using your nickname, you establish a private dialogue.

To leave private mode, type **/query**.

## rcp

The `rcp` command is a somewhat easier alternative to FTP as a way to transfer files on systems that support it. The `rcp` command is available on the same computers (mainly UNIX systems) that support `rlogin` and `rsh`.

To use the `rcp` command, the remote system must be set up so that it can automatically log you in to do the copy. For more information, ***see*** the discussion of `rlogin` later in this part.

In `rcp`, you refer to a file on another system with the system's host name, a colon, and the filename, such as `othersys:myfile`. If the file is in another directory, use the usual slash separator, such as `othersys:dirname/myfile`.

### Copying files from a remote computer

1. Type **rcp**, the source filename, and the destination filename. To copy a file named `mydata` from the host named `pumpkin` to the local machine and give that file the new name of `pumpkindata`, for example, you type **rcp pumpkin:mydata pumpkindata**.

2. `rcp` doesn't say a thing if the file transfers successfully, but you do see a message if there's a problem.

To copy a file if your username is different on the other system, you just type your username and @ before the host name, like this:

```
rcp steph@pumpkin:mydata pumpkindata
```

To copy to or from another user's directory on the remote computer (if the permissions allow you to do so), use a tilde (~) and use the username as the directory name:

```
rcp pumpkin:~tracy/somefile tracyfile
```

TIP

`rcp` is extremely taciturn, saying nothing at all unless something goes wrong. If you're copying a large number of files over a network, it can take a while (like a couple of minutes), so you may have to be more patient than usual while waiting for it to do its work.

### Copying all the files in a directory

To copy all the files from the home directory on the remote computer to the current directory on your computer, type **rcp**, the remote directory name, a period (which stands for the current directory), and the `-r` (for *recursive*) flag.

To copy all the files from the current directory on your local computer to the current directory on the remote computer, type **rcp**, a period (which stands for the current directory), the remote directory name, and the `-r` (for *recursive*) flag.

## rlogin and rsh

`rlogin` provides the same function as `telnet` (***see*** the `telnet` discussion later in this part), but the advantage of `rlogin` is that you can automatically log in to a different system. However, `rlogin` is not as widely supported as `telnet`. If `rlogin` doesn't work, use `telnet` instead.

### Connecting to a remote computer

To connect to another system by using `rlogin`, do the following:

1. Type **rlogin** and the name of the computer, as in **rlogin shamu**.

2. The remote system will ask you for your password unless you're set up for automatic login, as we describe below.

3. After `rlogin` connects to the remote computer, everything you type is sent to the remote computer and its responses are returned to your screen.

TIP

If your username on the other computer is different from your username on your own computer, type it after `-l`:

```
rlogin shamu -l king
```

***See*** the section "Logging in automatically by using rlogin and rsh" later in this part for how to arrange for automatic login.

`rlogin` may ask what kind of terminal you're using. If it makes a suggestion, accept it and then see what happens. Common terminal types are VT100, ANSI, and 3101.

## Disconnecting from a remote computer

To end an `rlogin` session, you log out by doing the following:

- The normal way to exit is to log out from the remote computer, usually by typing **logout** or **exit**.
- If the other end won't let go, press Enter, type **~.** (a tilde and a period), and press Enter again. `rlogin` disconnects and exits.

## Running commands on a remote computer by using rsh

`rsh` is a junior version of `rlogin` which runs one command at a time on a remote system. To use it, you must be set up for automatic login, as we describe in the next section.

1. Run `rsh`, giving it the name of the remote system and the command to run:

   ```
   rsh shamu who
   ```

   (This command runs the `who` command on a computer named `shamu`.)

2. If your login name on the other system is different from the one you use on your own computer, include that login name on the command line after `-l`:

   ```
   rsh shamu -l king who
   ```

On some UNIX systems, the name `rsh` runs a useless *restricted shell.* In that case, this command's name is `remsh` or `rshell`.

rsh doesn't properly run full-screen programs that take character-at-a-time user input, such as text editors like emacs or vi or mail programs like elm or pine. To run full-screen programs, use rlogin instead.

## Logging in automatically by using rlogin and rsh

You can arrange for the rlogin and rsh commands to log you in without asking for your name or password. If a group of computers is administered together, the group often has a shared user community, so anyone allowed to log in to one of the computers in the group can actually log in to any of the computers. To handle this case, a system file lists all the hosts whose users are equivalent to this one. On UNIX systems, this file is called /etc/hosts.equiv, and the file is called something similar on other machines.

For example, if machine abel has a hosts.equiv file that contains the name of machine baker, then anyone on baker can rlogin to abel by using the same username without giving a password.

If your system uses the NIS, which is a system that shares ID information among a group of computers, the system consults an NIS hosts.equiv database in addition to its regular file. To see the database, type

```
ypcat hosts.equiv
```

In the other situation, you have accounts on several hosts, but the accounts are not all under the same management. In that case, you arrange your own rlogin setup. Here's how:

1. On each machine, create a file called .rhosts on UNIX systems or just rhosts on others.
2. In this file, list all the other host computers on which you have accounts. Put your username on each system after the host name, separated by a space. For example, if your username is sam on systems Abel and Baker and tilden on system Clarissa, your .rhosts files should contain

```
Abel sam
Baker sam
Clarissa tilden
```

WARNING: Be sure your .rhosts file has protection mode 0600 so nobody but you can see your passwords.

# telnet

## Connecting to a remote computer

The `telnet` program lets you log in to and use other computers on the Net as if you were sitting in front of one of their terminals.

1. To run `telnet`, type **telnet** followed by the host name of the computer you want to log in to. Type the host name on the command line.
2. The `telnet` program connects to the remote system. In the process, it tells you the *escape character,* the character to press if you have trouble disconnecting from the remote computer later.
3. Log in to the remote system as if you were connected directly.

After you connect, the remote system may ask you what kind of terminal you're using. If you choose the wrong terminal type, the information on your screen will be scrambled. If `telnet` makes a suggestion, accept it and see what happens. Common terminal types are VT100, ANSI, and 3101.

## Disconnecting from a remote computer

To end a `telnet` session, you log out and end the connection by doing the following:

1. Log out from the remote system as though you were connected to it directly. `telnet` closes the connection and, on most systems, exits.
2. If the remote system won't log you out, try pressing the escape character (usually Ctrl+]). A prompt that says `telnet>` appears.
3. If you don't get the `telnet>` prompt in a few seconds, press Enter. The prompt should appear.
4. After the prompt appears, type **quit** and then press Enter.

   `telnet` closes the connection and exits.

Part VII

# Finding Resources on the Net

So many resources are available on the Internet that finding them can be harder than using them. This part describes ways in which you can search for and retrieve information on the Net by using the World Wide Web.

## In this part . . .

- Using Lynx to see the World Wide Web without pictures (but fast!)
- Using Netscape or Internet Explorer to see the World Wide Web in its full graphical glory
- Where to find useful information on the Internet

# Internet Explorer

Microsoft Internet Explorer is a Web browser that works on certain versions of UNIX (only Solaris, as of this writing). If Internet Explorer is installed on your system, it works similarly to Netscape (described later in this part), which we recommend you use instead. For information about Internet Explorer, see *The Internet for Dummies,* 5th Edition, or visit the `www.microsoft.com/ie` Web site.

# Lynx

The Lynx program lets you browse the World Wide Web, which is a hypertext system that links together many kinds of information all over the world. By displaying a Web document (or *page*) and selecting a highlighted topic on that page, you can move from page to page to find information.

Depending on your kind of terminal, links may be highlighted in bold or reverse video, or with a code number in brackets after the item. You can follow these links to see other information.

1. Type **lynx** at the shell prompt. The Lynx startup screen is displayed, containing several links to other resources.
2. Move the cursor to the desired link with the up and down arrow keys and then press Enter. (Use the up and down arrow keys even if the links are on the same line.) On a system that displays links as numbers in brackets, you can also type the number of the link you want and then press Enter.

If the page doesn't fit on-screen, press the spacebar or + to go forward or b to go back.

Web pages can include pictures. However, Lynx is a text-only program and cannot display pictures. Instead, it puts a note saying `[INLINE]` where each picture would have gone.

## Going directly to a page

If you know the name of a Web page, you can go directly to that page:

1. In Lynx, press g (as in *go*).
2. Type the name of the Web page and then press Enter. A typical Web address looks like this:

   ```
   http://net.gurus.com/
   ```

## Going back to a previous page

There are two ways to view pages you've already visited:

- ✦ To move to the last page you viewed, press the left arrow key.
- ✦ Lynx keeps a list of Web pages you have viewed in the past. An easy way of going to previously viewed pages is by using this History list.

  1. Press the Backspace key (some versions of Lynx say to use Delete, but they mean Backspace) or Ctrl+H. The History list appears.
  2. Depending on your system, use the arrow keys to select the page you want or press the number next to the desired page.
  3. Press Enter. Lynx displays the selected page.

## Searching within Web pages

1. In Lynx, type a slash (/).
2. Enter the word(s) that you want Lynx to find in the current Web page. Separate words with spaces.
3. Press Enter. Lynx moves to the first occurrence of the word(s).

## Key summary

| Key | Description |
|---|---|
| up arrow | Goes to the preceding screen. |
| down arrow | Goes to the next screen. |
| left arrow | Goes to the preceding link or page. |
| right arrow | Goes to the highlighted link or page. |
| Enter | Goes to the highlighted link or page. |
| (number) | Enters the number next to a link to go to that link or page. |
| space | Goes to the next screen. |
| / | Searches for text in the current Web page. |
| Backspace or Ctrl+H | Views the History list. |
| g | Goes directly to a page. |
| h | Views the Help screen. |

*(continued)*

| Key | Description |
|---|---|
| m | Goes to the main screen (the starting screen). |
| o | Changes Lynx options. |
| p | Prints the current page. |
| q | Quits Lynx. |

TIP

The keys used to enter commands may differ depending on your system and keyboard. If some commands don't seem to work properly, press o (as in *options*). Doing so displays an option screen that lets you change the keys you use to enter commands.

# Netscape

Netscape is a graphical Web browser which runs on an X workstation or terminal. Because it runs in a graphical environment, it can display pictures as well as text. Like Lynx, Netscape lets you surf the Web, moving from document (or page) to document by clicking hyperlinks. The commands given here are for Netscape Communicator, also known as Netscape Version 4.0.

TIP

Netscape Communicator 4.0 on UNIX works just like Netscape Communicator 4.0 on Windows or the Mac.

## Starting up

To start Netscape, type **netscape &** at the shell prompt. The *home page,* or starting point, appears. (The ampersand tells the shell not to wait for Netscape to be done.)

At the top of the screen are several buttons that you can click to move around the Web. You can also access the functions that these buttons provide by using the drop-down menu.

## Going to a new page

There are two ways to move from Web page to Web page:

- ✦ Click a hyperlink. *Hyperlinks* are words on a page that are either underlined or displayed in a different color than the rest of the text. Sometimes, you can click a picture to go to another page. The mouse pointer changes to a little hand when it's over a clickable link.
- ✦ Type the name of the Web site, as described in the following steps.

If you know the name of a Web site, you can go directly to that page.

1. Choose File⇨Open Page from the Netscape menu.
2. Type the name of the Web site and press Enter.

*URL* stands for *Uniform Resource Locator,* which is the type of address used on the Web. A typical URL looks like this:

`net.gurus.com/`

You can also click in the Location field on-screen and type the URL there.

## Going back to a previous page

There are two ways to view a page you've already looked at:

- To move to the last page you viewed, click the Back button at the top of the screen.
- Netscape keeps a list of Web pages that you have viewed in the past. An easy way of going to previously viewed pages is by using this list, or *History:*
  1. Choose Go from the menu. The History appears as a menu.
  2. Select the desired item.

## Finding places to go in Netscape

The Guide button on the Navigation Toolbar turns into a menu if you click and hold the mouse on it. (The Personal Toolbar located beneath the Navigation Toolbar duplicates this menu.) Here, you can find links to interesting Web sites, including

- What's New and What's Cool are lists of interesting pages compiled by the Netscape staff
- Lookup People and Lookup Yellow Pages let you search for e-mail addresses and telephone numbers of people and businesses

See "Research Indexes" later in this part for some recommended Web sites. For more information on Netscape, go to the `home.netscape.com` Web site.

## Printing a page

1. Choose File⇨Print from the menu. The Print window appears.
2. Enter the desired print command if it differs from the default. For example, you may want to print to a different printer than the one listed.

3. Click Print to print the document.

### Saving a file

1. Choose File⇨Save As from the menu. The Save Document window appears.
2. Select the directory in which you want to save the file.
3. Type a name for the file.
4. Select one of the three save options: plain text (without formatting); PostScript; or source (saves the text and the special HTML codes used to create the page).
5. Click Save to save the page to a file.

TIP

You can also save text from a page by copying and pasting. To copy text, click the left mouse button and drag it over the text you want. On some systems, you click the right mouse button to indicate the end of the range of text you're copying. Then switch to another window and press the middle button to paste the text you copied.

### Freeing disk space

WARNING

The Web page cache is not cleared when you leave Netscape, so it gets larger and eventually consumes a lot of disk space (usually 5 megabytes by default). You can clear the cache if you need the space back.

1. Choose Edit⇨Preferences from the menu.
2. Select Advanced/Cache tab in the window that appears.
3. Click Clear Disk Cache Now.
4. Click OK to confirm that you want to clear the cache.

### Quitting Netscape

To leave Netscape, choose File⇨Exit from the menu.

CROSS-REFERENCE

For more information on Netscape, see *The Internet For Dummies,* 5th Edition.

## Resource Indexes

Several good *search engine* Web sites allow you to search for topics or keywords throughout the Web or Usenet. These search engines have become the most efficient methods of searching for information on the Internet. Some of the most popular sites are

| *Name* | *URL* |
|---|---|
| AltaVista | www.altavista.digital.com |
| Deja News | www.dejanews.com |
| Excite | www.excite.com |
| HotBot | www.hotbot.com |
| Infoseek | guide.infoseek.com |
| Lycos | www.lycos.com |
| Northern Light | www.northernlight.com |
| Yahoo! | www.yahoo.com |

The Usenet archive at rtfm.mit.edu has useful information and references to archives elsewhere on the Net, including the FAQs (lists of frequently-asked questions and their answers) for most Usenet newsgroups. (See Part VIII for information about newsgroups.) It is indexed by newsgroup. There are two easy ways to get to it:

✦ FTP to rtfm.mit.edu, change the directory to /pub/usenet-by-group, and then go to the newsgroup you're interested in — for example, sci.med for information about medicine.

✦ Send an e-mail message to mail-server@rtfm.mit.edu consisting of the single word *help* to get started.

To find mailing lists (e-mail-based discussion groups and newsletters), visit the Liszt Web site at www.liszt.com.

For updates to this book, and other information about the Internet, visit our Internet Gurus Web site at net.gurus.com.

# Usenet Newsgroups

*Usenet,* also known as *network news* or *netnews,* is a gigantic bulletin-board system that's distributed worldwide. Usenet is made up of more than 10,000 *newsgroups,* each of which features a discussion on a specific topic. Several UNIX newsreading programs (including `trn`, `nn`, and `tin`) are popular. This part describes how to read Usenet newsgroups by using `trn`.

If you are using an X Windows GUI, several good X-based newsreaders may be available on your system; check with your system administrator. (Netscape Collabra is a newsreader that is bundled with many UNIX installations of Netscape. It works pretty much the same on UNIX as it does on Windows or the Mac.) The basic principles of using an X-based newsreader are the same as using `trn`, except that you click buttons with the mouse instead of typing cryptic one-letter commands.

## In this part . . .

- **Finding and subscribing to newsgroups**
- **Finding articles on specific topics**
- **Reading, posting, and saving articles**
- **Skipping over offensive articles**
- **Getting help**

# Netiquette: Avoiding Getting Flamed

Internet etiquette rules apply equally to e-mail and news articles — actually more for news articles, because far more people read them than read a piece of e-mail. Here are a few basic rules:

- Read the newsgroup for several days before making your first post so that you can get a feel for the group before jumping in.
- Don't post a follow-up to the whole newsgroup if the follow-up is intended only for the author of the original article.
- Be sure that each article is appropriate for the newsgroup to which you post it.
- Avoid posting a two-line follow-up that quotes an entire 100-line article. Edit down the quoted material so that your follow-up has more original material from you than quoted material.
- Don't forward personal e-mail messages to newsgroups without the author's permission.
- Most newsgroups have a periodic Frequently Asked Questions (or *FAQ*) message that answers many of the questions that you may need to ask. Check for a FAQ message before asking. (If you have access to the World Wide Web or FTP, many FAQ messages are available on the system `rtfm.mit.edu` in the directory `/pub/usenet`.)

# Reading Usenet Newgroups with trn

The `trn` program is one of the most popular UNIX newsreaders. The commands are all one letter long and not easy to remember, but `trn` is great for reading active newsgroups with lots of messages. It *threads* articles, that is, it organizes replies to appear after the articles they reply to.

## Starting your newsreader

TIP

In nearly all newsreading programs, you don't need to press Enter (or Return) after single-letter commands. Other commands require that you type a line of text, such as a filename or a newsgroup name, after the letter. In that case, you do press Enter to tell the program that you're done with the line of text. Be sure that you use either capital or small letters for one-letter commands *just as they are shown in the book* — the same letter can do different things depending on whether that letter is capitalized or not!

1. Run the `trn` program by typing **trn** at the shell prompt.
2. If the system says that the `trn` program is not found, ask your system administrator what other newsreaders are available.

When you run `trn` for the first time, it creates your `.newsrc` file and automatically subscribes you to some groups. You see something like this:

```
% trn
Trying to set up a .newsrc file-running newsetup...
Creating .newsrc in /usr/johnl to be used by news
programs
Done.
If you have never used the news system before, you
may find the articles in news.announce.newusers to
be helpful. There is also a manual entry for rn. To
get rid of newsgroups you aren't interested in, use
the 'u' command.
Type h for help at any time while running rn.
Unread news in general
        14 articles
(Revising soft pointers-be patient.)
Unread news in ne.food
        47 articles
Unread news in ne.forsale
        1177 articles
Unread news in ne.general
        268 articles
etc. ********  14 unread articles in general-read
   now? [+ynq]
```

Your newsreader now suggests a newsgroup for you to read.

`trn` keeps a list of the newsgroups that you're interested in (that is, that you're *subscribed to*). This list is stored in your .newsrc file; be careful not to delete it! If you're not interested in a newsgroup, you can *unsubscribe*. When new newsgroups are created, `trn` asks whether you want to subscribe to them.

To start, `trn` assumes that you're subscribed to some or all newsgroups, depending on how your news administrator configured the program. You unsubscribe to those newsgroups you don't care about. After the very first time you run `trn`, you don't see the first few lines of the preceding example; you see just the list of newsgroups to which you are subscribed and the number of unread messages in each. If you're subscribed to a whole bunch of newsgroups (more than about five), the program lists only the first few.

## Changing the order in which newsgroups appear

You can control the order in which `trn` presents groups. If you tell `trn` to present the most interesting ones first, you can move quickly through your favorite groups with the spacebar (to select a group to read) and n (to skip to the next group). When you run out of time, you can quit the program, skipping the less interesting newsgroups.

The first newsgroup you usually see is called *general;* this group is supposed to contain articles of general interest on your machine. In practice, newsgroup *general* tends to fill up with junk, and you should move newsgroup *general* toward the end of your list of groups. Here's how:

1. Press m (which stands for *move*).
2. If you want to move the current newsgroup, press Enter. To move some other group, type the group's name and press Enter. The program asks you where you want to move the group by displaying the cryptic prompt `[$^Lq]`.
3. If you want to see a list of the newsgroups to which you are subscribed (or have ever subscribed to), press Shift+L (some `trn` commands must be capitalized). You see a list of newsgroups.
4. Press the spacebar when the program pauses at the bottom of the screen. At the end of the listing, you see the same cryptic prompt.
   - To move the group to the end of the list (so that the group is the last one that you see), press $ (usually Shift+4).
   - To move the group to the head of the list so that that group is the first one that you see, press ^ (a carat, usually Shift+6).
   - To move the group so that it appears after another group, press + (usually Shift+=), type the name of the other group, and then press Enter.

## Choosing which new newsgroups to subscribe to

Because Usenet is exploding in popularity, a bunch of new newsgroups appear nearly every day. When you start `trn`, you see a list of the new newsgroups, and you have the opportunity to subscribe to them. Here's how:

1. Run `trn`. It asks a question such as this:

```
Checking active list for new newsgroups...
Newsgroup alt.comp.hardware.homebuilt not in
.newsrc-subscribe? [ynYN]
```

2. Press y or n to tell the program whether you want to subscribe to that particular newsgroup.
3. If you do want to subscribe to that newsgroup, the program then asks where in the list of newsgroups you want to see this new newsgroup, such as this:

   ```
   Put newsgroup where? [$^L]
   ```

4. Press $ to put the new newsgroup at the end of your list of newsgroups, or press ^ to put the newsgroup at the beginning, or press + followed by the name of an existing group to tell the program to put the new newsgroup after that particular existing group.

If you don't want to hear about any of the new newsgroups, press Shift+N to skip them all.

## Dealing with rot-13 articles

Offensive articles are sometimes encoded using *rot-13* (rotate 13), a simple coding system. If you encounter an article that contains gibberish, assume that the article has been encoded by someone using rot-13.

1. Decide whether you want to read the article. (You can usually tell what the subject is from the subject line, which is not encoded.)
2. Skip the article by pressing n, or press X to go ahead and pollute your soul.

## Dealing with shar files

Some messages contain groups of files, most often a group of C-program files in *shar* (*sh*ell *ar*chive) format. Extract files in this format with e in exactly the same way that you extract uuencoded files (***see*** "Dealing with uuencoded files" in this part).

## Dealing with uuencoded files

Some files contain encoded binary data, such as pictures or executable programs. Such messages contain lines that look like this:

```
begin plugh.exe 644
M390GNM4L-REP3PT45G00I-05[I5-6M30ME,MRMK760PI5LP
TMETLMKPYME0T39I4905B05Y0PV30IXKRTL5KWLJR0JTOU,6
  P5;3;MRU050I4J50I4
```

This type of format is called *uuencoded* format.

Before you can use this information, you must *extract* it:

1. Display the text of the article.
2. Press e and then press Enter. If you want the data someplace other than your `News` directory, type the directory name after the e.
3. If the file is large and is split across multiple messages, press e in each message in order.

## Exiting the newsreader

When you're bored by reading messages from computer nerds from all over the world or realize that it's almost 5:00 and you haven't gotten any useful work done all day, it's time to leave your newsreader.

To do so, press q. Depending on where in the program you are, you may have to press q two or three times.

## Finding articles on specific topics

`trn` can search for articles that contain a specific word, phrase, or part of a word in the subject line.

1. While you're reading a newsgroup, press a slash followed by the characters you want to search for. For example, to find information about chickens, type **/chickens**.
2. The program displays the next article that contains the characters you type. If the program doesn't find an article that contains those characters, it tells you so.

If you want to scan backward through the articles, press ? rather than / before the characters you want to search for.

You can tell the program what to scan: either just the headers or the whole article (which takes longer). To scan only the *From* lines (which say who posted the article), type

`/pattern/f`

where *pattern* is the characters you're searching for.

To scan only lines in the header, but not lines in the text of the articles, type

`/pattern/h`

To scan entire articles (which can take a while), type

`/pattern/a`

To scan articles that you've already read, type

`/pattern/r`

To match the capitalization of the pattern you're searching for, type

`/pattern/c`

## Finding a newsgroup

When `trn` asks whether you want to read a newsgroup, you can read the articles in a different newsgroup instead. To read the messages of a particular newsgroup, you use the `g` (`goto`) command.

1. When the program asks whether you want to read a newsgroup, press g (and don't press Enter).
2. Type the name of the newsgroup.
3. Press Enter. Your newsreader subscribes you to the newsgroup.

If you unsubscribed to a newsgroup and want to resubscribe to it, this command does the trick.

You can also search for newsgroups by name with the `l`(`list`) command.

1. When the program asks whether you want to read a newsgroup, press l (and don't press Enter).
2. Type the name of the pattern that you want to find in a newsgroup name.
3. Press Enter. Your newsreader presents you with a list of newsgroups containing the pattern. You can then subscribe to the group with the `g` command.

TIP

To find a newsgroup that interests you, read either `news.announce.newgroups` or `news.announce.newusers` newsgroups; both contain complete listings of all the newsgroups.

## Getting help

`trn` doesn't have the world's finest online help, but their online help is sometimes better than nothing. There are three separate help pages. If `trn` is asking you whether you want to read a newsgroup, you'll see a list of the newsgroup selection commands. While you're looking at the list of threads in a newsgroup, you see the list of thread-selection commands. While you're reading articles, you see a list of commands that control the way articles appear.

1. To see the newsreader's online help, press h. You see a terse listing of commands, one per line.
2. The listing of commands is too long to fit on one screen. Press the spacebar to see the next page.

## Posting a new article

You can start your own thread by posting an article. Just make sure that the article is on an interesting topic, that the newsgroup didn't just discuss that topic at length last week, and that you have your facts straight.

TIP: Before posting an article, be sure that you have read the newsgroup for at least a week so that you know which topics the newsgroup is discussing and what the style of the newsgroup is; that you have read the newsgroup's FAQ; and that you are calm or (even better) in a good mood.

1. Within `trn`, enter the newsgroup of interest.
2. If you're in the thread-selection screen, press Enter to go to the article-reading screen.
3. Press j to tell the program that you're not reading any articles.
4. Press f (as though you were writing a follow-up article to something).
5. The program asks whether you're sure that you want to write an article. If you are sure, press y and then press Enter.
6. When prompted, enter a new subject for the article.
7. Write the new article the same way that you'd write a follow-up (as described in the section "Replying to and following up an article").

TIP: If you're not running `trn` at the moment, you can use the `Pnews` command to post news directly. At the command prompt, type **Pnews** followed by the name of the newsgroup to post to. Then follow the directions given in this part for posting an article.

WARNING: Some newsgroups are *moderated,* which means that articles are not posted directly as news. Instead, articles are e-mailed to a human or robot moderator who actually posts the articles if they are appropriate to the group. Moderators, often being human, do not process items instantaneously, so processing items can take a day or two. If you write an article for a moderated group, the news-posting software tells you that your article is being mailed to the moderator.

## Reading articles

After you choose a newsgroup to read (by pressing the spacebar when `trn` asks whether you want to read the messages in the group), `trn` shows you the first screen of the first unread article. You can read each article that you haven't read yet, skip over articles that look boring, reply to messages, print them, or save them.

A group of messages that have the same subject is called a *thread.* If a subject looks boring, you can tell `trn` to skip entire threads.

1. To read the messages in a newsgroup, press the spacebar when `trn` asks whether to read them.

   You see the first message that you have not read, such as this:

   ```
   general #6281
   From: Admin
   Re: Disk space
   Organization: I.E.C.C.
   Date: Sat Aug 8 06:48:03 1998
     The disks are nearly full again. Please
     delete unneeded files, or we'll delete some
     for you.
     (Yes, that's a threat.)
     - Your friendly system manager
   End of article 6281 (of 6282)-what next? [npq]
   ```

2. If the article is too long to fit on-screen, press the spacebar to see the next screen of the article.

3. To see the next article in this newsgroup, press n. If you don't feel like reading any of the unread articles in the newsgroup, press c to *catch up* — pretend that you've read all the articles. If you have finished reading articles in this newsgroup, press q.

The first line of the article tells you the name of the newsgroup *(general)* and the message number within the group (6281). The last line tells you how many articles are in the newsgroup (6282, in this case) and which one you are looking at again (6281, which means that one more unread message is in this newsgroup).

TIP

After you get the hang of it, you'll mostly press the spacebar to go to the next article or newsgroup, n to skip an article or newsgroup, and k to skip a group of articles (as described in the next section). Until you prune the set of newsgroups you're subscribed to down to something reasonable, you may also be hitting u frequently to get rid of the large majority of groups that you don't want to read.

| Key to Use While Reading an Article | Meaning |
|---|---|
| Spacebar | Read the next page of the current article or the next unread article. |
| B | Back up a page. |
| n | Skip to the next article. |
| k | Kill this article and any others with the same title. |
| K | Same as k; also enter the title in the killfile so that the title is rekilled each time you enter the group. |
| q | Stop reading this group. |
| c | Catch up (pretend that you've read all articles in this group). |
| u | Unsubscribe to this newsgroup. |
| s*file* | Save article to a file named *file.* |
| \|lpr | Feed article to command *lpr* (this method is the easiest way to print an article). |
| /*xyz* | Find the next article whose title contains *xyz.* |
| = | Show titles of unread articles. |
| Ctrl+L | Redraw the screen. |
| Ctrl+R | Restart the current article (redisplays the first page). |
| X | Unscramble a rot-13 message (not for the squeamish). |
| e | Extract uudecoded or shar file. |
| e*dir* | Extract into directory *dir.* |
| h | Show extremely concise help. |

## Replying to and following up an article

You can write a response to an article in two different ways:

- ✦ You can send e-mail, known as a *reply,* to the article's author. The other folks in the newsgroup won't see your reply because your reply is a private e-mail message.
- ✦ You can write an article of your own to the newsgroup at large; this process is known as *posting a follow-up article.* Post a follow-up article only if you're sure that most of the people in the newsgroup may find your response interesting.

## Sending an e-mail reply

1. While the original article is still open, press r. If you want to include some or all of the text of the article in your reply, press R instead.
2. `trn` starts a text editor (usually `vi` or `emacs`) with a skeleton of the reply message already provided. If you press R, the text editor includes a copy of the original article with your reply.
3. Type your reply. If you're starting your message with the original article, delete the irrelevant parts of the article.
4. Save the file and exit the text editor.
5. `trn` asks whether you want to send, abort, or edit the response. To send the message, press s. If you change your mind, press a to abort the reply and not send anything.
6. The program then asks whether it should add your standard signature (stored in your file `.signature`). Press y unless you have already signed the article.

## Posting a news follow-up

1. Press f to send a follow-up. If you want to include some or all of the text of the article in your follow-up, press F instead.
2. The program asks whether you're sure that you want to send a follow-up to the whole Net. If you're sure that's what you want to do, press y.
3. `trn` starts a text editor, with a skeleton of the follow-up message already provided. If you press F, it includes a copy of the original article.
4. Type your follow-up. If you started with the original article, delete the irrelevant parts.
5. Save the file and leave the text editor.
6. The program asks whether to send the follow-up. Press y to send the follow-up or press a to abort and not send it.

WARNING: All news articles that you send, including follow-ups, automatically add your `.signature` file. Don't put in the signature yourself, or your signature will appear twice.

## Saving an article

Just like mail messages, newsgroup articles can be saved in files.

1. To save an article that you're reading, press s followed by the name of the file in which to save it; then press Enter.

2. If the file doesn't already exist, `trn` asks whether to make the file a mailbox. To make the file a mailbox, press y.

TIP

If you don't specify a directory, `trn` saves articles in files or mailboxes in the `News` subdirectory in your home directory. You can put articles in other directories by specifying the directory name, but `News` is usually as good a place as any.

## Selecting newsgroups to read

After you begin running `trn` or `rn`, you choose which newsgroups to read (unless you decide to follow all 25,000 of them). When you see a message such as `23 unread articles in soc.couples-read now? [+ynq]`, press one of the keys listed in the following table.

| Key | Meaning |
|---|---|
| Spacebar or y | Enter the next group that has unread articles (described in "Reading articles" earlier in this part). |
| + | Display a list of the threads that contain unread articles. |
| n | Skip this group for now (see "Skipping over a newsgroup" later in this part). |
| u | Unsubscribe from this group so that you won't see it any more (***see*** "Unsubscribing to a newsgroup" later in this part). |
| g | Go to a different newsgroup; type the newsgroup name after the g (***see*** "Finding a newsgroup" earlier in this part). |
| q | Leave `trn`. |
| p | Go to the previous group with unread news. |
| h | Show extremely concise help. |
| Ctrl+L | Redraw the screen. |

## Selecting the threads that you want to read

After you tell `trn` to enter a newsgroup, so many articles may be in the newsgroup that even killing and junking them still leaves too many to read. Instead of reading all the articles, you can select only those subjects that you *do* want to see.

`trn` has a feature called *thread selection* that makes this selection easy. Follow these steps to use it:

1. Enter the desired newsgroup by pressing + (instead of the usual spacebar or y). You see a screen such as this:

```
general                              14 articles
a 0000-uucp(0000)    3  New mail paths
b 0000-Admin(0000)  10  backup
d Chet Arthur        1  System will down to
   clean hamster cages -
Select threads - All [Z>] -
```

The first line tells you the newsgroup's name and the number of articles in the newsgroup. The following lines list the threads with a one-letter identifier (for example, *d*), the author of the first article in the thread *(Chet Arthur),* the number of messages in the thread *(1),* and the subject *(System will down to clean hamster cages).* The last line asks which thread you want to read.

2. Press the appropriate letters (the one-letter identifiers) to select the threads that you want. To select a range of threads, press the letter of the first thread followed by a hyphen and the letter of the last thread. A plus sign appears next to each selected thread.

3. To go to the next page of threads, press > (right-arrow key).

4. To start reading the threads that you've selected, press Z or Tab.

TIP

If you want to read all the threads on the current screen, simply press Z or Tab without selecting any of the threads.

To *junk* (arrange never to see) the threads that aren't selected, press D. The most effective way to pick just the articles of interest is to select the interesting threads on each screen by using the key letters and then press D to quickly skip the rest of the threads on that screen.

TIP

The spacebar is set up to pick the command that you're most likely to want at the end of each screen. If another screen of threads is available, the spacebar does the same as > to go to the next screen. On the last screen, pressing the spacebar does the same as pressing Z to start reading articles. Each `trn` prompt shows you suggested commands in square brackets, and pressing the spacebar always takes the first suggestion.

| *Thread Key Selection Letter* | *Meaning* |
|---|---|
| Spacebar | Read the next page of the table of contents or start reading selected articles if no more threads are in the table of contents. |

*(continued)*

| Thread Key Selection Letter | Meaning |
|---|---|
| D | Start reading selected articles; mark unselected articles as read. |
| Z | Read selected articles. |
| */xyz* | Select articles whose titles contain *xyz.* |
| *c-g* | Select articles *c* through *g* in the current table of contents. |
| c | Catch up by pretending that you've read every article in the group. |
| h | Show extremely concise help. |
| q | Leave this group. |

## Skipping over a newsgroup

When `trn` asks whether you want to read a newsgroup now, you can skip over the newsgroup just this once. To skip a group for the time being, press n to say, "No, don't read it now." You remain subscribed to the newsgroup.

## Skipping an uninteresting or offensive article

Often, you find an article to be uninteresting enough that you want to skip it, skip all the replies, and perhaps skip every future reply as well.

- ✦ To skip (kill) this article and all others with the same subject, press k (lowercase k).
- ✦ To curse this subject permanently and skip it in the future as well, press K (capital K).
- ✦ To skip (junk) the rest of this thread, even if the subject changes, press J.

Pressing K adds a command to one of your *killfiles;* that is, files in your News subdirectory that store information about what types of articles you want to skip in the future. Press Ctrl+K to edit the killfile for the current newsgroup.

## Skipping unread articles

When you're reading articles in a newsgroup, press c (for *catch up*) to mark all the unread articles in the newsgroup as read. If hundreds of unread articles are in a newsgroup that you follow, you may want to mark them all as read so that you don't have to face them.

### Unsubscribing to a newsgroup

When `trn` asks whether you want to read a newsgroup, you can tell `trn` that you never want to hear about the newsgroup again. To unsubscribe from a group, press u.

## Understanding Newsgroup Names

Usenet newsgroups are named according to a hierarchy. They consist of several parts separated by dots — for example, `rec.food.chocolate`. The first part of the name (`rec`, in this example) determines which *hierarchy* the newsgroup belongs to and describes the general subject area. The following table lists the most widely read subjects.

| Newsgroup Name | Description |
|---|---|
| `comp` | Topics having something to do with computers. |
| `sci` | Topics having something to do with the sciences. |
| `rec` | Recreational groups (about sports, hobbies, the arts, and other fun endeavors). |
| `soc` | Social groups (both social interests and plain socializing). |
| `news` | Topics having to do with Usenet itself. A few groups contain general announcements; otherwise, they're not very interesting unless you're a Usenet addict. |
| `misc` | Miscellaneous topics that don't fit anywhere else. (The ultimate miscellaneous group is called `misc.misc`.) |
| `talk` | Long arguments, frequently political. Widely considered totally uninteresting except to the participants. |
| `alt` | Unofficial *alternative* newsgroups, ranging from the topical to the weird to the totally stupid. |

Regional and organizational hierarchies also exist. For example, the `ne` hierarchy is for topics of interest to New England, `ny` is for New York, and `ba` is for the San Francisco Bay area. Universities and other organizations big enough to have their own Usenet communities often have hierarchies of their own, such as `mit` for MIT.

***See*** *The Internet For Dummies*, 5th Edition (published by IDG Books Worldwide, Inc.) for more information about Usenet newsgroups.

# Techie Talk

**absolute pathname:** A pathname that tells you how to find a file by starting at the root directory and working down the directory tree. Absolute pathnames begin with a slash (/).

**address:** The name you use to say who is supposed to receive an electronic-mail message. An electronic-mail address consists of the person's user name and, if on a different computer than you are, the name of the computer.

**Alt key:** If your keyboard has an Alt key, it is used as a Shift key; it does nothing on its own. To use the Alt key, hold it down, press and release another key, and release the Alt key. To press Alt+A, for example, hold the Alt key, press and release the A key, and release the Alt key. Simple. Lacking an Alt key, you can usually press Esc and then the letter to get the same effect.

**anonymous FTP:** Uses the FTP file transfer program and the Internet to copy files from other computers to your own. It is *anonymous* because many computer systems allow anyone to log in and transfer files without having accounts (user names) on the computer. You type **anonymous** as the user name and your electronic-mail address as the password.

**application:** A program that really gets some work done. Some programs just organize the computer, get its parts talking to each other, and do other housekeeping chores. Applications do real-world work, such as word processing or accounting.

**argument:** Something that appears on a command line after the command. Suppose you type this line:

```
cp old.file new.file
```

In this command, `cp` is the name of the command or program, `old.file` is the first argument, and `new.file` is the second argument.

**ASCII (American Standard Code for Information Interchange):** ASCII defines the codes that the computer uses internally to store letters, numbers, punctuation, and some control codes. Almost all UNIX computers use ASCII (except for some IBM mainframes).

**background:** UNIX can run many programs at the same time. If a program runs behind the scenes — that is, with no interaction with you — it runs in the background.

**backslash (\):** UNIX uses a backslash to set off otherwise-special characters. In the UNIX shell, for example, * is a literal asterisk (a plain * matches every file in the current directory); \\ is an actual backslash. Windows and DOS users tend to type backslashes by mistake because DOS and Windows pathnames use backslashes where UNIX uses slashes (/).

**bang (!):** In UNIX-ese, an exclamation point is called a *bang.* The C shell command `!!`, for example, which repeats the last command, is pronounced "Bang! Bang!" Try this with your small children — they'll love it.

**BASH:** The Bourne Again shell, the GNU re-creation of the Bourne shell. Program name is `bash`.

**bin:** A directory that contains programs. Your home directory probably has a subdirectory named `bin`. The system has directories called `/bin` and `/usr/bin`.

**bit:** A tiny piece of information that can be either a 1 or a 0. Bits tend to get lumped into groups of eight bits, called *bytes.*

**Bourne shell:** The Bourne shell is the original, classic UNIX shell. It prompts you with `$`. Its program name is `sh`.

**browser:** Program that displays World Wide Web pages.

**BSD UNIX:** A version of UNIX developed and distributed by the University of California at Berkeley. BSD stands for *Berkeley Software Distribution.*

**buffer:** A small storage area in which information is stored temporarily until it is needed. Lots of things have buffers: printers frequently have buffers to store the next few lines or pages to print; `emacs` (a text editor) refers to its copies of the files you are editing as buffers.

**byte:** Eight bits in a row. That is, a series of eight pieces of information, each of which can be either 1 or 0. A little higher math tells you that there are 256 different combinations of eight 1s and 0s. (256 is 2 to the 8th power.) There are, therefore, 256 different values for a byte of information. Most computers use a system of codes called *ASCII* to determine what each pattern means. ***See also*** ASCII.

**C:** A programming language, invented at the same time as UNIX, in which nearly all UNIX programs are written. C is a great programming language for lots of reasons. C programs look a lot like random punctuation strewn across the page. Luckily, you do *not* have to know C to use UNIX, so we don't write about it anywhere else in this book.

**C shell:** The C shell is a UNIX shell written to look like the C programming language, sort of. It prompts you with %. Its program name is `csh`.

**CD-ROM:** A computer disc that looks just like a music CD but contains data rather than music.

**CDE (Common Desktop Environment):** In X Windows, a program that combines a *window manager* with a set of menus and buttons so that many common UNIX functions can be done with mouse clicks instead of typed commands.

**click-to-focus:** A system that GUIs (*graphical user interfaces*) use to control which window you are working in. When you want to move to a different window, move the mouse and click the new window to tell the GUI that you want to use that window.

**client:** In X Windows, a program that does real work (as opposed to a program that displays the results on-screen).

**client-server architecture:** A system (used by systems including X) that enables a program (the *client*) to run on one machine while the program that displays its results (the *server*) runs on another machine. In X, the client often runs on a remote machine while the server runs on the computer sitting on your desk, managing your screen and keyboard. Confusingly, the term "client-server" is also used in the database world and the Internet to mean when a presentation or analysis program (the client) runs on your local machine and the database engine or other information-providing program (the server) runs on another, remote computer.

**command:** What you type to get UNIX to do something. Actually, the *UNIX shell* listens to the commands you type and tries to execute them. Some commands are things the shell knows how to do. Other commands are separate programs, stored in files on the disk. When you type a command, press Enter or Return at the end of the line.

**command mode:** When you use the `ed` or `vi` text editors, you are in either command mode or input mode. In command mode, whatever you type is interpreted as a command.

**compression:** A way to shrink files so that they don't take up so much space. File-compression programs that do this include `gzip`, `compress`, and `pack`. To uncompress a compressed file, use `gunzip`, `uncompress`, `unpack`, or `zcat`.

**Control key:** The key on the keyboard labeled *Control* or *Ctrl.* It is used as a Shift key; it does nothing on its own. To use the Ctrl key, hold it down, press and release another key, and release the Ctrl key. To press Ctrl+D, for example, hold down the Ctrl key, press and release the D key, and release the Ctrl key.

**.cshrc:** The file in your home directory that the C shell runs automatically when it starts.

**current directory:** ***See*** working directory.

**current job:** The job most recently started or stopped. When you use the `jobs` command to list jobs, the current job is marked with a plus sign (+).

**daemon:** A process that runs around on its own to see to some housekeeping task. Your computer, or some computer on your network, has a printer daemon whose job is to print things waiting in the print queue.

**directory:** A collection of files with a name. A directory can be compared to a file folder that contains one or more files. Directories can also contain other directories. You can think of a directory as a work area because one directory is always the current *working directory.* Directories, particularly directories contained in your home directory, sometimes are called *subdirectories,* for no good reason.

**DOS:** An operating system patterned in some ways after UNIX. DOS runs on PCs.

**dumb terminal:** A terminal that has no processing power of its own. It usually doesn't have any nice options either, such as mice or screens that can do graphics.

**editor:** ***See*** text editor.

**electronic mail (or e-mail or email):** Typed messages delivered by a computer network rather than on paper.

**Enter key:** In a UNIX shell, pressing Enter means that you have just typed a command and want UNIX to do it. In a text editor, pressing Enter means that you want to begin a new line. The Enter and Return keys usually do the same thing (your keyboard may have one, the other, or both).

**Escape key:** The key labeled *Escape* or *Esc*. What this key does depends on the program you're using.

**executable file:** A file that UNIX can run like a program. An executable file can contain binary machine instructions that the computer knows how to execute, or it can contain a *shell script* (a list of UNIX shell commands) that UNIX knows how to execute.

**external command:** A command that the shell doesn't actually know how to do. Instead, a program is stored in a file with the same name as the command. If you type the `ed` command (to run the dreadful `ed` editor), for example, UNIX runs the program contained by a file named `ed`.

**file:** A bunch of information stored together with a name. A file can contain text, programs, or data in any format.

**file system:** A set of files stored on a disk or on one partition of a disk. A file system has one root directory that contains files and subdirectories. These subdirectories can, in turn, contain files and other directories.

**file transfer:** Copying files from one computer to another.

**filter:** A small UNIX program used with input or output redirection. The most commonly used filters are the `more` and `sort` commands.

**flag:** ***See*** option.

**folder:** A file that contains electronic-mail messages that you decided to save.

**foreground:** A program currently capable of talking to your terminal.

**fork:** When UNIX starts a new process, it does so by cloning an existing process. The cloning process is known in UNIX-ese as *forking*. Pronounce it carefully to avoid embarrassment.

**Front Panel:** Window that appears along the bottom of the screen when you are using CDE.

**FTP:** A file-transfer program that enables you to log in to another computer and transfer files to or from your computer.

**FVWM:** (*F*ine? *F*eeble? No one really knows.) *V*irtual *W*indow *M*anager. A popular window manager commonly used on free UNIX systems, such as Linux, and on some commercial systems.

**GNU:** A free software version of many parts of UNIX written by the Free Software Foundation (FSF). For more information, check out their Web site at `http://www.gnu.org`.

**GUI:** A *g*raphical *u*ser *i*nterface. GUIs let you use the computer by pointing at things with a mouse rather than typing commands. The most common UNIX GUI is the X Window system. GUIs sometimes are called *windowing systems.*

**header:** The first part of an electronic-mail message that contains the address of the sender and recipient, the subject, and lots of other stuff that's less interesting.

**hidden file:** A file with a filename that begins with a period. These files do not appear on regular `ls` directory listings. Use `ls -a` to include hidden files in a directory listing.

**hyperlink:** Words on a Web page that you can click (or select) to display another related Web page.

**home directory:** The directory you start in when you log in, usually a subdirectory of `/usr`. You should keep your files in your home directory or in subdirectories of your home directory.

**icon:** A cute little picture used in conjunction with a GUI. A well-designed icon is supposed to be an obvious, unmistakable symbol of whatever it stands for, occupy much less space than do the equivalent words, and be cute. In practice, many icons are peculiar little pictures with no obvious meaning.

**inbox:** ***See*** mailbox.

**incremental backup:** A backup copy of only the files that have changed since the last full backup.

**input mode:** When you use the `ed` or `vi` text editor, you are in either command mode or input mode. In input mode, whatever you type is entered into the file.

**Internet Explorer:** Microsoft's Web browser, available for Solaris.

**I/O:** Input and output, that is, information going into or coming out of a program, computer, or other computer-type device.

**I/O redirection:** ***See*** redirection.

**job:** A program you start from the shell that can start, stop, and move between the foreground and background.

**K (also KB or kilobyte):** A measure of memory or disk size that is 1,024 bytes of information. This number happens to be 2 multiplied by itself 10 times — a nice, round number for computers.

**kill:** To stop a process from running.

**kludge:** Something that works but that the author is embarrassed about. Rhymes with "huge," not with "fudge." Some people spell it *kluge,* and we're sure that they too can learn to live productive and useful lives.

**Korn shell:** An enhanced version of the Bourne shell. For your purposes, it's mostly like the Bourne shell and prompts you with a `$`. Its program name is `ksh`.

**line editor:** A text editor that deals with text one line at a time. Line editors were great back when terminals printed on paper instead of displaying information on a screen. Most modern text editors let you see and work with the file an entire screen at a time. The `ed` program is a line editor; we recommend that you use something better.

**link:** An additional name for a file. When you create a file, you create its contents, which are stored on the disk, and you give it a name, which is stored in a directory. There is a connection between the filename and its contents. You can create additional filenames and connect them to the same contents by using the `ln` command.

**Linux:** A free version of UNIX originally written by Linus Torvalds in Finland and now developed by a cast of thousands all over the world, connected by the Internet.

**local mount:** Logically connects several disk drives on the same machine so that they appear as one directory tree.

**log in:** To identify yourself to the UNIX system and provide your password so that UNIX believes that it's really you and lets you use the computer. You have a login ID, or user ID, or user name — that is, the name by which UNIX knows you. When you finish working, you log out.

**.login:** A hidden file containing a shell script. If you use the C shell, this script runs automatically every time you log in.

**login directory:** ***See*** home directory.

**Lynx:** A Web browser that runs under UNIX. Lynx doesn't display any pictures, but the text looks great.

**MB (also M or megabyte):** Measure of memory and disk size that is 1,048,576 bytes, or 1K times 1K, or 2 multiplied by itself 20 times.

**mailbox:** The directory in which the electronic-mail system puts your incoming mail.

**mailing list:** E-mail–based discussion group or newsletter.

**man page:** A short file of information about a UNIX command. The `man` command displays manual pages about all UNIX commands and a few other topics, although they usually are written in a hopelessly technoid style.

**Meta key:** If your keyboard has an Alt key, it may act as the Meta key. If not, press the Escape key to achieve the same effect. The effect depends on the program you are running. `emacs` uses the Meta key for many commands.

**MIME (Multipurpose Internet Mail Extensions):** A way to attach any kind of file to an e-mail message.

**Motif:** A GUI based on X Windows and distributed by the Open Software Foundation.

**mounting directories:** Logically attaching the root directory of one file system to some other directory so that you can treat all the files in the file system as though they were subdirectories. Mounts can be *local* (on the same machine) or *remote* (on a different machine).

**netiquette:** Rules of polite behavior for sending electronic mail.

**Netscape:** Graphical Web browser. Also called Netscape Navigator or Netscape Communicator.

**network:** A bunch of computers connected by some combination of cables, phone lines, satellites, or whatever. A network enables computers (and their users) to share information and peripherals. Networks are especially good for sharing printers (so that you can all share one good-but-expensive laser printer) and for passing around electronic mail.

**NeXTstep:** An extremely cool GUI that runs on NeXT machines.

**OPEN LOOK:** A GUI based on X Windows and developed by AT&T. Most people use Motif instead.

**operating system:** A special program that controls the way the computer, keyboard, screen, and disks work together. UNIX is an operating system, as is DOS.

**option:** Also known as a *flag* or a *switch,* an option is something that tells UNIX how to do a command. You type an option on the command line after the name of the command, separated from the command by a space. Options usually begin with a hyphen (-).

**parent directory:** The directory that contains the current working directory. That is, the current working directory is a subdirectory of the parent directory.

**password:** A secret series of characters known only to you. You type your password when you log in.

**pathname:** Instructions for how to get to a file. An *absolute pathname* (which starts with a slash) tells you how to find a file beginning at the root directory and working down the directory tree. A *relative pathname* tells you how to find the file starting where you are now.

**peripheral:** Something that lets the computer communicate with the outside world — mainly with you. The keyboard, screen, mouse, printer, and modem all are peripherals.

**permissions:** Whoever has the right to look at, change, and execute stuff in a file or directory.

**pipe:** The | character, used to redirect the output of one command so that it becomes the input of another command.

**pointer-focus:** A system that GUIs use to control which window is active. To tell the GUI which window you want to work in, just move the mouse pointer to that window.

**policy independence:** A characteristic of X Windows in which windows can look and act any way the software developers want. This idea is the converse of the idea that, if all the windows on your screen look and act in a similar way, they are easier to use.

**portable software:** Programs that can be run on many different kinds of computers. UNIX is portable because it runs on an amazing number of different types of computers, including PCs, workstations, minicomputers, and mainframes.

**PostScript:** A computer language spoken by printers and the programs that communicate with these printers. PostScript enables printers to print a wonderful array of characters in all kinds of sizes and shapes (as well as pictures). When a program wants to print something on a PostScript printer, it has to send a PostScript program that tells the printer how to print the stuff.

**process:** A running program.

**.profile:** A hidden file that contains shell commands. If you use the Bourne or Korn shell, this file runs automatically every time you log in.

**prompt:** The character or characters displayed whenever UNIX (or some other program) is waiting for you to type something. The two common UNIX prompts are $ (if you use the Bourne or Korn shell) or % (if you use the C shell).

**queue:** A waiting line, just as in real life. The most common queue is the print queue, in which the output of `lp` or `lpr` commands waits in line to get printed.

**read-only:** A file that can be read (copied and so on) but not written (changed). UNIX has a system of permissions that enables the owner of the file, the owner's group, or all users to have (or not have) permission to read, write, or execute the file.

**real-time:** Right now, as opposed to whenever the computer gets around to it.

**redirection:** To hijack the output of a command, which is usually on-screen, and put it somewhere else (this process is called *output redirection*). Alternatively, you can use information from somewhere else as the input for a command (called *input redirection*) rather than take the input from the keyboard. To redirect the output of a command to a file, use the > character (or >> to append the output to an existing file). To redirect the input of a command from a file, use the < character. To redirect the output of one command to become the input to another command, use the pipe (`|`) character.

**remote login:** Logging in to another computer from your own computer. This process requires that your computer be on a network or have a phone connection.

**remote mount:** Using NFS to connect directories from disk drives on other machines so that they appear as part of your file system.

**request ID:** The ID number of a print job as it waits in the print queue for the printer daemon to get around to printing it. You need to know the request ID if you want to cancel printing when, for example, the output is horribly fouled up and wasting lots of paper.

**Return key:** When you use a UNIX shell, pressing Return means that you just typed a command and want UNIX to do it. When you use a text editor, pressing Return means that you want to begin a new line. The Enter and Return keys usually do the same thing (your keyboard may have one, the other, or both).

**RFS (Remote File System):** Like NFS, a program that lets you treat files on another computer in more or less the same way as you treat files on your own computer.

**root:** ***See*** superuser.

**root directory:** The main, top-level directory on a disk. All the files on the disk are in either the root directory or a subdirectory of the root directory (or a sub-subdirectory and so on).

**screen editor:** A text editor that deals with text an entire screen at a time. The `vi` and `emacs` programs are screen editors.

**script:** ***See*** shell script.

**search engine:** Web site that allows you to search for topics or keywords throughout the Internet.

**search path:** A list of directories in which UNIX looks for programs.

**server:** There are lots of kinds of servers. A *database server* is a program that maintains a database and both provides information from it to client programs and accepts updates to it from client programs. A *file server* is a computer or program that stores files for use by other computers or programs. A *Web server* is a program that stores Web pages and provides them to Web browsers on request. A *news server* is a program that stores Usenet newsgroup articles and provides them to news clients. A *mail server* is a program that handles incoming or outgoing mail. You get the idea. ***See also*** X server.

**shar message:** An electronic-mail message that contains a shell script that re-creates one or more files when you run it. A clever way to send nontext files through electronic mail.

**shell:** A UNIX program that listens for commands that you type and tries to execute them. There are several UNIX shells, including the Bourne shell, Korn shell, C shell, and BASH.

**shell script:** A file that contains a list of UNIX shell commands. You can *run* a shell script, thereby telling UNIX to execute every command in the list.

**slash:** The / character that UNIX uses in pathnames. A / by itself, or at the beginning of a pathname, means the root directory of the file system. Slashes are used also between one directory name and the next, and between the directory name and the filename in long pathnames. A slash (/) is not the same as a backslash (\).

**soft link:** A link that contains the name of another file, which may be on another file system. A soft link makes it look as though the file from the other file system is in a directory on your own file system. Also called a *symbolic link.* ***See also*** link.

**subdirectory:** ***See*** directory.

**superuser:** The user name with which you can do all sorts of dangerous things to the system, including creating new user names and installing new hardware and software. Also known as *root.* With luck, you don't know the password for the superuser. If you do, *use it carefully.* The system administrator really should be the only person who logs in as the superuser.

**SVR4:** Release 4 (the final version) of UNIX System V from AT&T. Contains more features than any six people would ever want to use.

**switch:** ***See*** option.

**symbolic link:** ***See*** soft link.

**system administrator:** The person whose job it is to keep the computer, and possibly the network, running.

**System V:** A version of UNIX developed and distributed originally by AT&T, later by UNIX System Labs, later by Novell, and now by SCO and Hewlett-Packard.

**telnet:** A program that enables you to log in to another computer from your computer.

**terminal:** A screen and keyboard connected to a computer somewhere else. The terminal doesn't run UNIX and all those neat programs itself; it just lets you use the computer that does.

**terminal emulator:** A program that enables a big, powerful computer to act like a dumb, cheap terminal. Commonly, a PC can run a terminal emulator so that you can use another computer running UNIX.

**terminal output stop mode:** A terminal setting in which a background job stops if it tries to send anything to your screen. Use `stty tostop` to turn this setting on.

**text editor:** A program that lets you create files of text and edit (or change) them. The most common UNIX text editors are `ed`, `vi`, and `emacs`.

**text file:** A file that contains lines of text. All the stuff in a text file must be ASCII characters — no bizarre control codes, data, programs, or the like. You can use the `cat` command to look at a text file on-screen. If a file looks like it was written by Martians when you use the `cat` or `more` command to view it, it's not a text file.

**text formatter:** A program that reads text files and creates nice-looking formatted output. The most common UNIX text formatters are `troff`, `nroff`, and `TeX`.

**UNIXWare:** Novell's version of UNIX. Descended from SVR4.

**URL:** Uniform Resource Locator, the address of something (usually a Web page) on the Internet.

**Usenet:** A very large, very informal, very disorganized network through which many megabytes of news, rumor, and gossip are distributed every day.

**user name:** The name by which UNIX knows you. You enter this name when you log in. Also known as your *user ID* or *login ID.*

**utility:** A small, useful program. UNIX comes with some utilities, such as `diff` and `sort`.

**uucp:** The mostly-obsolete UNIX-to-UNIX copy program. One of the ways that mail, Usenet news, and random files can be sent between computers.

**uuencoded file:** A binary file that has been cleverly converted to a string of text characters so that it can be sent by e-mail or Usenet news. Useful for sending images or programs to other people.

**virtual memory:** A sneaky trick by which UNIX pretends to have more memory than it really does. When you're not looking, UNIX copies information from memory to the disk to free up space in memory. When you need the information on disk, UNIX copies it from the disk back into memory. Virtual memory is generally invisible, except when a program uses it too enthusiastically; then the computer spends all its time copying stuff back and forth to the disk and no time doing useful work, a condition called *thrashing*. Virtual memory isolates one program from another, so that if one program goes crazy (or goes West), other programs are not affected.

**wildcard:** A special character that acts like a joker when used in filenames or pathnames. UNIX has two: * and ?.

**WIMP:** *W*indows, *i*cons, and *m*ouse *p*ointing. ***See also*** GUI.

**window:** A rectangular area of the screen in which a program displays something. If you use a GUI, you can have several windows on-screen at a time, each displaying a different program.

**window manager:** A program (such as FVWM and the Motif manager) that gives the screen the overall look of a GUI.

**wizard:** A person who knows more about UNIX than is really healthy. Encourage wizards to get outside once in a while, but make sure that they don't sneak out with a laptop and cellular modem!

**word processor:** A program that lets you create documents — files that contain text, pictures, and formatting codes. UNIX word processors include WordPerfect and those bundled with ApplixWare and StarOffice.

**working directory:** The directory you are working in. The `pwd` command tells you your working directory.

**workstation:** A computer with a big screen, a keyboard, and a mouse. If it runs UNIX, it's called a workstation; if it runs DOS, it's called a PC. And if it runs MacOS, it's called a Mac.

**X server:** A program that draws the pictures and displays the text on-screen if you use X Windows or a GUI based on X Windows. The X server runs on the computer on your desk. The client program can run on any computer that can reach your X server over the network.

**X terminal:** A terminal that can run X so that you can use X Windows or Motif. It has a little computer in it to do the X stuff.

**X window system (or just X):** A GUI designed at MIT and based on X. It is the defacto standard windowing system for UNIX systems.

**XENIX:** A version of UNIX developed by Microsoft and now maintained and distributed by SCO (Santa Cruz Organization).

# Index

## Symbols



## A



## B

## D



## E

## I



## J



## K



## L

## M



## N



## O

## P



## Q



## R

## S

## T



## U

# IDG BOOKS WORLDWIDE BOOK REGISTRATION

**Register This Book and Win!**

## *We want to hear from you!*

Visit **http://my2cents.dummies.com** to register this book and tell us how you liked it!

- Get entered in our monthly prize giveaway.
- Give us feedback about this book — tell us what you like best, what you like least, or maybe what you'd like to ask the author and us to change!
- Let us know any other *...For Dummies*® topics that interest you.

Your feedback helps us determine what books to publish, tells us what coverage to add as we revise our books, and lets us know whether we're meeting your needs as a *...For Dummies* reader. You're our most valuable resource, and what you have to say is important to us!

Not on the Web yet? It's easy to get started with *Dummies 101*®*: The Internet For Windows*® *98* or *The Internet For Dummies*®, 5th Edition, at local retailers everywhere.

Or let us know what you think by sending us a letter at the following address:

*...For Dummies* Book Registration
Dummies Press
7260 Shadeland Station, Suite 100
Indianapolis, IN 46256-3945
Fax 317-596-5498

...FOR DUMMIES™
BESTSELLING BOOK SERIES FROM IDG